S0-BCW-927

Breaking Into Article Writing

Breaking Into Article Writing

■■■■

Sondra Forsyth Enos

■■■■

Publishers   THE WRITER, INC.   Boston

Copyright © 1988
by SONDRA FORSYTH ENOS

"The New Romance," "Lights, Camera, Action," and "Animal Antics," by
Corrine Clements, pseud., are reprinted by permission of *Ladies' Home
Journal.*
Copyright © 1984, 1985, by Meredith Corporation. All rights reserved.

All rights reserved, including the right to reproduce
this book or parts thereof in any form.

Library of Congress Cataloging-in-Publication Data

Enos, Sondra Forsyth.
  Breaking into article writing / by Sondra Forsyth Enos.
    p.   cm.
  ISBN 0-87116-150-8
  1. Authorship.   2. Journalism—Authorship.   I. Title.
  II. Title:
  Article writing.
  PN145.E64   1988   87-34813
  808'.02—dc19   87-34813   CIP

Printed in the United States of America

*For Clive, Christopher and Stacey
and for my mother and my late father*

CONTENTS

Acknowledgments

I would like to thank the four editors-in-chief for whom I have served as a staff member: Myrna Blyth, *Ladies' Home Journal;* Helen Gurley Brown, *Cosmopolitan;* Lenore Hershey, *Ladies' Home Journal;* and Barbara Tober, *Bride's*. Each in her own way offered encouragement and advice, allowing me to improve my writing and editing skills over the years.

Profound thanks also to Sylvia K. Burack, editor-in-chief of *The Writer*. As the editor of this book, she has been a constant source of encouragement and wisdom. Without her enthusiasm for the project, her patience and her invaluable input, I would not have been able to produce the manuscript.

My appreciation as well to every editor for whom I have worked as a free-lance writer, and to every writer who has worked for me while I was an assigning and line editor. Each interchange has been a valuable learning experience and I am grateful for having had the opportunity to collaborate with so many fine professionals.

I also owe a debt of gratitude to Mary B. Lott, who was my ninth grade English teacher, and to Opal Milligan, who was my twelfth grade English teacher. Both of them recognized and nurtured my burgeoning interest in writing.

Thanks also to my family for supporting me in this endeavor. Special thanks to my daughter, Stacey, whose astute comments and questions have been immeasurably helpful during the writing process.

Introduction

WHENEVER I SPEAK to a writer's group, the question of how I got my start inevitably comes up. Did I go to journalism school? Take a mail-order course? Major in English? Finagle an introduction to a top editor through a friend? Get an agent? Live in Manhattan?

No, on all counts. I never took any journalism or writing courses, I majored in Spanish, I didn't know anybody who could introduce me to an editor, I still don't have an agent, and I grew up in Michigan. How, then, did I become a free-lance writer and eventually a magazine editor?

What I did was exactly what I'm going to teach you how to do. I broke in "over the transom." That is, I sent an unsolicited query with a stamped, self-addressed envelope to a magazine for which I wanted to write—*Gourmet*, to be precise—and got a "go-ahead on speculation" answer. This is how beginners are asked to work, meaning that the editor reserves the right to reject the piece without paying anything. Nonetheless, editors do not request to see a manuscript unless they firmly believe the story will fill their needs. Anyway, you have to start somewhere, so please do take that first "go-ahead on spec," just as I did. In fact, you may have to write "on spec" for some time. Only after you've become established and have clips to prove what you can do, will you get firm assignments with a "guarantee" or "kill fee" of 15% to 25% of the promised fee, even if the editors choose not to buy your piece. At that point, you will also be in a position to request that the magazine buy First North American Serial Rights, meaning that rights will revert to you after the magazine publishes your piece. (Selling "all magazine and serial rights throughout the world" means that the publication will retain the rights to your piece.)

In my case, *Gourmet* bought that first article for the princely sum of $300. Well, that seemed like a lot of money to someone in her early twenties in 1966. Anyway, the sale was joyous proof to me that a person does not need any special credentials to be a free-lance nonfiction writer, and I began to generate and market my work in earnest.

As it happened, I was right about not needing credentials, but in the ensuing years, both as a writer and as an editor, I came to realize that my first sale, a personal experience piece about a taverna in a remote village on the island of Crete, was something of a fluke. I had a story no one else could offer, the writing was acceptable, with editing, and that was that. But few writers manage to make a career out of writing personal experience articles. Most article writing turns out to be very hard work, involving research, interviews, and careful crafting to suit the "voice" of a particular magazine. I had the privilege of learning this from both sides of the desk, so to speak. For the record, besides free lancing, I've been the Articles Editor at *Bride's*, a Features-Text Editor at *Cosmopolitan*, and Articles Editor, then Executive Editor, at *Ladies' Home Journal*. Now I have what I consider the choicest post of all. I'm Editor-at-Large for the *Journal*, meaning that I write by-lined pieces, but I still have time for "my own" work—like this book, which I've been wanting to share with you. I know you love to write, and I'm sure you'll agree with the motto on the coffee mug that sits on my desk: "Success is doing what you love." I can't promise you fame and fortune, but I *can* help you become a selling writer. Maybe you won't break into the major markets right away (or ever), but there are hundreds and hundreds of potential places for you to submit your work—magazines that will publish your pieces, give you by-lines, and send you checks. That's my idea of success, and I'll wager that it's yours, too. And even though I'm not a buying editor anymore—but just one of the pack, right out there competing for assignments—I honestly hope you'll end up giving me a run for my money. The very best of luck!

—S.F.E.

Breaking Into Article Writing

 **1**

That's A
Great Idea!

OBVIOUSLY, THE FIRST STEP in article writing
is finding something to write *about*. Once
you've become an established nonfiction writer,
editors may make a habit of calling you up and
offering you assignments based on ideas cooked
up in editorial meetings, but until that millennium
comes, it's up to you to originate fresh story ideas.
In Chapter 3, I'll explain how to present those
ideas in what is called a "query letter"—a snappy,
attention-getting synopsis of the piece you plan to
write—that the "slush" readers on the magazine's
editorial staff will pass on to senior editors. The
"slush pile" is the heap of unsolicited mail that
arrives daily at editorial offices, and the first readers want nothing so much as to discover new
writers so their editors will notice what splendid
judgment they have and henceforth promote
them. This factor, coupled with the dismal but
inescapable truth that most of the slush is riddled

with misspellings, dangling participles, and other horrors, should work in your favor if you take pains to make none of these mistakes. In other words, despite the volume of slush, if your entry is at all appealing, well-written, and neatly presented, you do have a fighting chance.

But as I said, it's no good knowing the technique of query writing if you don't have a clue as to how to come up with ideas. And originating good—let alone great—ideas is not easy. To begin with, you need to understand the difference between a *subject* and an *article idea*. A subject is a broad topic of possible discussion—such as, say, in-law relationships. One could produce a six-part series on the various aspects of in-law relationships. Therefore, letting an editor know that you would like to write a 3,500-word magazine article on in-law relationships will probably get you an instant rejection slip. You need to look at the specific aspects of in-law relationships, as well as the article needs of the magazines for which you might wish to write, and draw up a list of ideas. As a rule of thumb, if you can come up with a title or a lead sentence or both, you probably have a viable idea. Here are some examples:

IDEA	PUBLICATION
"The Other Man in Her Life: How to Cope with Your Future Father-in-Law"	*Esquire, Playboy, GQ*

"The Other Woman in His Life: How to Cope with Your Fiancé's Mother"	any bridal magazine
"The Girl That He Married: Getting Along with Your Son's Wife"	magazines for middle-aged readers and mature readers
"Home for the Holidays: How to Survive (and Even Enjoy) a Houseful of 'His and Hers' Relatives"	any traditional women's magazine or parenting magazine
"Thy Brother's Wife: A Single Woman Loses a Brother, Gains a Sister-in-Law, and Lives to Tell about It"	*Cosmopolitan, Glamour, Mademoiselle*
"When Grandma Baby-sits"	*Working Mother, Modern Maturity,* any parenting magazine, *Redbook*

Each of these titles represents a single aspect of the general topic of in-law relationships, one that could reasonably be developed into an article directed at the readership of a particular magazine or groups of similar publications. If you proposed one idea to the right magazine, there would be a good chance of getting a positive response—not an immediate rejection—from the editor, and there are variations of these subjects and themes that could be proposed to different publications, small and large.

On the other hand, there would be no guarantee that you'd get a go-ahead, either. Why? The titles I suggested are fairly routine, the sort of articles magazine editors run periodically as part of the backbone of their publications. Consequently, there is a strong possibility that these or similar titles are already in the works or in the inventory of the magazines at which you're aiming your ideas. Editors of the largest magazines have scheduled idea meetings during which they decide on the basic "stories," which is what editors call nonfiction pieces. Editors must usually assign these basic pieces to keep the magazine's larder well stocked, and enable them to plan several issues in advance. During those meetings, since editors and assistants read extensively (every major newspaper and magazine is read by at least one staff member on a regular basis), ideas based on current events and research are also discussed. This means that if there is a surge of interest in adult children of alcoholics, or AIDS among heterosexuals, or contraception dispensed by public schools, or "frozen embryo" babies, most editors will assign a piece to an established writer before a new free-lance writer can even get a query letter into the mail.

This last point, incidentally, explains why it may sometimes seem as though an editor has "stolen" your idea—having rejected a perfectly good query of yours and then run a similar piece a few months later by a known writer. You can be absolutely sure, though, that no editor ever "steals" ideas. First of all, editors don't need to. Except for an occasional brainstorm, ideas for magazine articles tend to be abundant and redundant. It's the execution, the writing, the presentation, that make the difference.

Based on what I've said so far, you can see why your ideas, even if they're on target, may not get you a go-ahead. As a new writer breaking into the business, you'll have to face that fact. But don't be discouraged. There definitely are ways to get a foot in the door. Here are the three most reliable:

• *True-life dramas.* Many markets, including religious and denominational magazines and the top-paying major women's magazines, gobble up these gripping and informative articles about human courage. What's wonderful for you is that you may well be in a position to offer a unique piece on a subject that editors have no way of knowing about until you tell them. They do their best to keep abreast of the world by reading *The New York Times, The Chicago Tribune, The Los*

Angeles Times, The Washington Post, and even a number of smaller papers. But you may have access to, say, the *Toledo Blade,* or better yet, the *Fremont News Messenger,* both published in your native Ohio. On a given day, you might find an item about local high school students who have organized fund raisers in order to help a crippled Amerasian orphan . . . or a mother who gave a kidney to save her desperately ill baby . . . or a stray dog who curled around a lost toddler on a freezing Christmas Eve, saving the little one from death by hypothermia . . . or a six-year-old who gave a playmate the Heimlich maneuver, preventing the child from choking on a jelly bean . . . or a young woman who danced at her wedding, sixteen years and endless hours of painful therapy after having a severed leg reattached by microsurgery. Any one of those items is the kernel of a first-rate magazine drama, and since you are right there in Fremont, Ohio, with access to the interviewees, you have a good chance of getting a crack at the piece.

• *Write about what you know.* If you are an expert at anything—needlepoint, nursing, dog grooming, gardening, antique collecting, doll houses—there is probably a market for articles about your specialty. This may not be a high-paying market, but you'll be polishing your craft and getting some tear sheets. After all, not every piece you sell, even after you're an established writer, has to go to a major publication. In fact, lots of writers make a career of writing for specialty markets. The pay is often modest, though many inflight, regional, and city magazines pay better rates than you might think, and these publications are often more receptive to new freelance writers than major magazines are.

Yet while we're discussing writing about what you know, I want to proffer an important caveat. Your personal experiences, unless they are extraordinary, are not necessarily the stuff of which articles are made. Your operation, your divorce, and your weight loss, however significant to you, will not be of interest to a magazine unless the operation is the first of its kind, your divorce was from a closet transsexual, or your weight loss was in excess of 200 pounds. There are exceptions, of course. Breast cancer, tragic though it is, has been written about in the first person so many times, by Betty Rollin and Betty Ford and a host of lesser-knowns, that most staff slush readers will automatically reject a breast cancer query. But the writing *can* make the difference. If you are so eloquent, so inspiring, so human or universal, so clearly a cut above the rest, your story may still be purchased. All I'm saying is that by and large, you must be objective about judging the interest value of your own experiences, and learn to think like an editor. Don't listen to every friend and relative who gushes, "Oh, you should write about that!" Ask yourself whether you would write about it if it had happened to someone you don't know, or ask yourself whether you would buy it if you were an editor with a limited purchasing budget.

There are hundreds of publications, both magazines and newspapers, that welcome personal experience essays, but, obviously, writing about what you know has limitations. Your expertise about rose growing or needlepoint will certainly not garner you sufficient assignments to keep you writing even on a part-time basis, and your personal experiences are probably not earth-shattering enough or unique enough to warrant many major pieces. Even if you become a master of the personal or opinion essay, there wouldn't be much of a market for your work. So what now? It's time to try the third way to break in:

• *Write about what you don't know.* I mean, of course, that you should become an investigator and a researcher, making it your business to learn about a subject that intrigues you in general but one that is unfamiliar to you. I, for one, have written pieces on topics as varied as the impact of the media on youngsters today . . . the dilemmas a woman faces when she goes back to work before her baby's first birthday . . . the best way to make your dreams come true . . . the secret life of "latch-key" children . . . the history of the dance department at the University of Wisconsin . . . shopping tips for travelers to Egypt . . . how families cope with unemployment . . . how to overcome fatigue. And while many free lancers develop specialties—medical issues, financial writing, child care, travel—a good many make a career of constantly casting about for fresh areas of interest. As someone breaking into the article writing business, you will probably find that doors open more quickly when you offer one of the first two types of pieces I've mentioned—the true-life drama or the personal expertise piece. Even so, a well-researched, sparkling query in this third category could certainly get you a go-ahead on spec or an assignment. And in the long run, you'll definitely need to know how to handle the "write about what you don't know" article. However, before we go on to the question of how to craft the query that will make the editor sit up and take notice, I want to allay any fears you might have about trying to break into article writing if you don't live in or near the Big Apple. . . .

2

But I'm From Kalamazoo

D̲O YOU THINK OF NEW YORK as the center of the publishing world? If you do, don't be daunted by that idea! There are writers in every suburb, town, and hamlet from coast to coast who have more work than they can handle. You do not have to live in Manhattan to succeed in magazines. For one thing, I've already pointed out that your hometown newspapers are rich sources of true-life dramas otherwise unknown to Manhattan-based editors and writers, and this fact can be a big plus when you're trying to break into the major markets. Beyond that, don't forget that there are literally thousands of magazines based all over the country: Besides the magazines based in New York City, there are several major publications in other large cities. To name a few, *Playboy* (Chicago), the *Los Angeles Times Magazine* (Los Angeles), *Better Homes and Gardens* (Des Moines, Iowa) and *Smithsonian* (Washington, D.C.). All pay top rates and will consider queries from free-lance writers. Yet while my philosophy is that new writers should certainly "shoot for the moon," trying out ideas on the major markets first, a lot of effort should also go toward writing for the vast field of lesser-known regional and special interest magazines. I have right here on my desk a sheaf of special market reports from various issues of *The Writer*, which list excellent publications based in such diverse places as Odgen, Utah; Harrisburg, Pennsylvania; Indianapolis, Indiana; Rockville, Maryland; Topeka, Kansas; Greendale, Wisconsin; and Mission Viejo, California. You can be sure that these and other markets are hungry for material, and if you make yourself known to them as well as to the big-time "books" (editorial jargon in major magazine editorial circles for "magazines"), you can manage an ongoing article writing career, whether full- or part-time, from a kitchen table in Kalamazoo or a den in Des Moines as easily as from a penthouse on Park Avenue.

When it comes to writing for major markets, writers who live within easy commuting distance of Manhattan have a slight advantage over writers from Kalamazoo or Albuquerque: They are available for "story conferences" and "rewrite conferences" pretty much at an editor's whim. Editors of magazines outside New York City tend to work with authors via the mails, but New York editors in general find it easier to deal with writers who can conveniently arrange to come in to the editorial offices for one-on-one meetings, particularly when it comes to ideas that are generated in-house.

So where does that leave you when it comes to breaking into the major markets? Chin up. Along with those local papers full of true-life dramas, you have something even more important going for you. You are in a position to generate your own ideas, again and again, because you live in "readerland"—the real world, where the daily lives of your family and your neighbors can inspire you. New York editors will be the first to tell you that as New Yorkers they sometimes find it difficult to keep their fingers on the pulse of the country, and that they honestly yearn for the input of writers who truly understand the concerns and joys of the good people who buy their magazines. Are you a man in Muskegon who doesn't just read *Field and Stream* but who lives for the outdoor life? The editors of that venerable magazine, based in New York City, want to hear from you. Are you a single working woman in Milwaukee? *Cosmopolitan* needs your help! Are you a high school teacher in Richmond, Indiana, who knows what today's teens are really like? Shoot some queries straight to *Seventeen*.

Ah, but I know there is still one question lurking in the back of your mind. You're wondering whether you need a literary agent. The answer is a simple "no." Very, very few magazine articles are sold through agents, even to the top markets, except for those that come from established authors of nonfiction books who have asked their agents to handle their short pieces as well. However, even book authors often choose to market their own articles. Why? They know that whether a writer has an agent or not, he needs to establish a working relationship with the magazine editors he writes for. Editors know what their readers want, what "mix" of articles they need, and what style and taste and length suit their pages. So take a tip from the pros. Stop worrying about getting an agent, and concentrate on developing a rapport with your editors. Learn how to shape your prose to fit their requirements, and you'll have an excellent chance of succeeding in magazines. In Chapter 13, I'll give you some tips on how you can nurture the special and vital relationship between editor and writer, whether you live in New York or North Dakota. But first, let's get past the pep talk, roll up our sleeves, and get on with the hard part—the how-to chapters that will give you the skills you need to produce first-rate magazine articles for today's markets.

3

What Is A
Query Letter?

LET'S SAY THAT YOU HAVE never been published, and you live in Appleton, Wisconsin. You want to break into article writing, and you have an idea for a piece on helping a child deal with the untimely death of a significant person in his or her life. You're neither a psychiatrist nor a social worker, just an ordinary person interested in this topic, for whatever reason. What now?

Your first step is to select "target markets"—those that would logically print a piece like the one you want to write—by referring to an annual market guide such as *The Writer's Handbook* (Sylvia K. Burack, editor, Boston: The Writer, Inc.). In reference books like this, you'll find the names of the editors to whom you should write, the length requirements for manuscripts, and the pay scales. Next, read several issues of your potential targets—in our sample case, religious magazines, parenting magazines, major and smaller women's magazines. (Many magazines are in your library, indexed in the *Readers' Guide to Periodical Literature*. Smaller, specialized magazines may not be found in libraries and are often difficult to find on newsstands, too. But the editors will usually send you sample copies free or for a small fee, on request. This service is commonly mentioned in the market guides.)

Now you're ready to pitch your piece, preferably to one market at a time. Multiple queries, at least to the major magazines, are really not a good idea unless the piece is timely. Smaller magazines, on the other hand, are more receptive to multiple queries, but you should tell the editors that you have sent the query to several editors at once. Editors don't like spending time considering your query, only to learn unexpectedly that you've accepted an offer from a competing magazine in the same field. This may seem unfair, but that's simply the way it is. (The trick is to have plenty of queries on different topics out to different markets at any given time, so you'll always have enough work and won't be waiting for that one story to click somewhere.)

All right. Let's say you've decided to aim for the biggest check you can get by selling your story to a major women's magazine called *Today's Parents*. (I made this magazine up just for didactic purposes.) Should *Today's Parents* reject your query, you can always try a more modest-paying magazine such as *The Episcopalian* or *Marriage & Family Living*.

First of all, do *not* try to skip the query letter by phoning the editor, unless you've written for the magazine before. After all, he has no idea whether you can write, not having seen anything on paper, not even a splendid letter to your Aunt Gertrude, let alone a query letter.

What is a query letter, anyway? It is a one- or two-page summary of your proposed article, showing that you have the style, the skill, and the necessary access to experts or authorities to write it. A new writer, eager to prove his talent, often wants to go beyond the editorial requirements and send a completed manuscript, but that's almost as bad as phoning an editor about an idea. For one thing, editors receive a lot of unsolicited mail and there's precious little time to read whole manuscripts. For another, looking at the situation from your point of view as a writer, why go to the trouble of researching and writing an entire piece on, say, lower back pain, when an editor may already have a piece on that subject or may have assigned a similar article to one of the magazine's regulars—meaning that even if your piece is just fine, it won't be bought? I'd say the only exceptions to the rule about querying first and not sending manuscripts are fillers, humor pieces, and "think" pieces—that is, opinion essays. Fillers (household hints, amusing anecdotes, light verse, how-to tips) are so short that it's best just to write them. Humorous or opinion pieces are so personal, and so dependent on each writer's particular gift and slant, that an editor simply can't predict the outcome from a query. But for all other nonfiction topics—reportage, child care, psychological self-help, medical, true-life dramas, how-to, personal experience, and so on—a good query is required.

There are many ways to go about writing a query, but I believe the most effective letter begins with a "grabber"—a titillating paragraph that might even be the lead to your article. Certainly, avoid the stiff format of an ordinary business letter, as in "I am interested in writing an article for your magazine on the topic of helping a child cope with the death of a relative or close friend." You are not writing to an insurance company, after all, but to an editor who wants to know whether you've got the knack. Far better to catch the editor's attention with something like:

> Jennifer Wilson is an eight-year-old charmer with enormous brown eyes, blond pigtails and a fair share of freckles. Like her third-grade classmates, she is learning about American Indians and memorizing her multiplication tables. She's a budding gymnast, and she likes to make clothes for her dolls. To a casual observer, then, Jennifer is a normal little girl. But those close to her know that she is wrestling with one of the gravest traumas a young life can sustain: the recent death of her mother.

Now that you've piqued the editor's attention, he will go on reading, so you've cleared the first hurdle. Your next job is to convince him that you can deliver all the elements of a first-rate article. Let me list them and then give you an example of what the body of the letter ought to look like:

1. Give statistics or expert quotes showing that the problem of children coping with the untimely death of family members and other important people in their lives is widespread enough to deserve discussion. Explain that your article will also help children deal with the even more common problem of the predictable but still devastating death of grandparents.

2. Let the editor know that you are prepared to substantiate and enliven your article with case histories—that is, anecdotal passages with quotes from people who have experienced whatever it is you are writing about. There are three ways to accomplish this:

a. *Interview people who agree to have their real names published*, and who may also agree to supply photographs or submit to photography sessions. This is the ideal, and is most easily accomplished when you are asking people to say what they would say in ordinary conversation anyway. For example, I once did a piece on how the media affect today's youngsters, and I got a number of mothers and fathers (neighbors of mine, cousins of friends in the Midwest, a writer I met when I was in Seattle once, and so on) to give taped interviews over the telephone, and to agree to have their names published with their quotes. People said such obvious and innocuous things as, "I limit my children's TV viewing to one hour a day, and I monitor which shows they watch," or "I read reviews before I take my kids to the movies, and even then, I'd yank them out of the theater if anything offensive came on the screen." In this case, I simply taped the interviews, with the interviewees' permission recorded at the beginning, and then wrote up the quotes practically verbatim, editing out a few "ums" and "ahs" and repeated phrases. I did not use a printed release form, although this can be an extra precaution and there would be no harm in doing so. Of course, if you interview people about a controversial topic, release forms are mandatory. (A sample release form appears at the end of this chapter.) I also did not allow the interviewees to see my manuscript or my galleys (proofs ready for the printer), since the people were not quoted extensively, nor portrayed in any way that could be construed as negative. Nonetheless, at major magazines, even articles such as this one are read by a staff libel lawyer and occasionally a recommendation for a change is made.

b. *Interview people who ask that their names and other details be changed to conceal their identities* and indicate this either in the text or in a footnote. This approach is common when the topic is sensitive and personal, such as marital and sexual problems, substance abuse, sexual abuse, domestic violence, compulsive disorders (kleptomania, nymphomania, bulimia, compulsive gambling or shopping), and mental or emotional illness. I would suggest giving each interviewee a fictitious first name ("Carol") or first name and surname initial ("Carol P.") or title and surname initial ("Mrs. P"). In order to preserve the character of your interviewee, choose a name that is similar in tone to the real name—"Peggy" for "Bonnie," "Elizabeth" for "Catherine," "Joe" for "Mike," "James" for "David."

Similarly, change occupations, but keep them within the same socioeconomic group, making a waitress into a repairman, a receptionist into a typist or secretary, a doctor into a lawyer, the owner of a hardware store into the owner of an auto parts shop. Also, selectively change or omit other details, such as color of hair and eyes, name of hometown or college attended, number and gender of children or siblings, provided that such changes will not affect the story. Also, definitely have your interviewees sign release forms. Once again, there is no need to allow the people you interview to see your manuscript, although you may do so if you wish, with the written proviso that you are under no obligation to make changes.

c. *Use quotes you hear (or overhear) in real-life conversations.* When I was doing a piece on working mothers, I not only interviewed people who agreed to be quoted, but I also became an inveterate eavesdropper. I caught exchanges between women at the supermarket, on the commuter train, in office corridors, in line for the bank machine. I either made mental notes, or actually jotted quotes down in my notebook as I heard them (in a bus, plane or restaurant) or shortly after hearing them, and I gave them anonymous attributions such as "said one overwrought young mother as she stood in the checkout line of a 24-hour supermarket at 10:00 p.m. on a Sunday evening."

This last technique is valid, but should not be your sole method of gathering anecdotal material. Do not be tempted to sit at your desk and make up quotes that you imagine people would say regarding your topic, and don't merge a little of one person with a little of another person for a "composite" case history that more neatly serves your purposes than anything you have managed to dig up in the real world. Quite simply, if you want to make cases up from scratch, write fiction. Remember the uproar over the *Washington Post* reporter whose Pulitzer Prize was revoked when it was discovered that the main character in her piece, "Jimmy," an eight-year-old heroin addict, was a well-crafted figment of her imagination? True, it's not likely that you would get caught if you made up an anonymous quote, but I hope this bit of journalistic laziness would be on your conscience. In the case of interviews with people who give their names, editors will ask for telephone numbers so facts can be verified. If you have given them fictitious case histories, they'll either send you back to the field or kill the piece. While I hesitate to sound cranky, I ought to mention that editors will find it hard not to remember you as being inexcusably unprofessional.

3. To help the editor understand the scope of your piece, indicate what each case history will illustrate. Let's say Jennifer's mother died of cancer, so this little girl gives you the opportunity to talk about the death of a parent as well as about the problem of witnessing a long, progressive illness. Or if Kevin's revered soccer coach was killed in an automobile accident, the boy opens up a discussion of children losing important adults— "heroes," in a way—other than family members, and he also sets the stage for a look at the problem of unexpected death. Or Kirsten's younger sister died of leukemia, so she's your jumping-off point for a section on the special problems of losing a sibling. Perhaps another child's best friend died, and that presents the opportunity for discussing other problems. Just show that you have a thorough but manageable story in mind, one that can be competently told in about 3,000 words.

4. Explain that you will contact the appropriate experts for interviews: In our sample case, these experts would include pediatricians, child psychologists, hospice workers and others who work with the terminally ill, clergy, and authorities on death and dying. Do some preliminary research in the library, and give the names of respected people in the fields you plan to cover. Don't worry about eventually getting through to the top experts. If you get a go-ahead from a magazine, that will open the door for you. And I'm not just talk-

ing about major markets. If you want to write for specialized markets—*Chess Life* or *Scale Woodcraft* or *Yoga Journal*—you'll find that you'll easily get interviews with the most important people in those fields.

In the meantime, by listing the recognized authorities, you've showed that you're up on your topic. If at all possible, magazine editors want quotes from the reigning experts in whatever subject area you're writing about, so take the time to find out who those headliners are and mention that you are going to get their views. By the way, don't choose to interview *your* child's pediatrician, *your* child's school psychologist, and *your* minister—or your hometown chess champ, woodcraftsman or yoga instructor—simply because they're easily accessible. No matter how knowledgeable these people are, unless they are widely known in their fields, they aren't the ones to approach for interviews. (The obvious exception, of course, is when you are writing for a regional or local publication, in which case you would not only want to interview the people right in your own backyard, but you might do a whole personality profile on a particularly colorful character.)

5. If pertinent, you might want to try to get some celebrity interviews as part of your article. In our sample case about a child losing a friend or relative, Christa McAuliffe's family and colleagues would seem an ideal choice. (See Chapter 4 for detailed information on how to approach celebrities.)

6. Mention whether you plan to add any service information. Boxes listing the names and addresses of support groups or books or government pamphlets pertaining to the topic often run alongside the appropriate article.

7. Sign off. I am personally opposed to the often recommended closer, "I can have this piece ready within six weeks." Of course you can, if you're any good. I also object to "May I have this assignment?" That sounds so pushy and canned, somehow. I'd rather read something original and sincere, such as: "I'm confident that the proposed article will touch the hearts of all who read it, and more important, fill a real need for information about this sensitive topic."

Now, let's see how these points ought to be handled in a brief, rejection-resistant query:

Martin Jones
123 Some Street
Appleton, Wisconsin 54914
June 20, 1988

Leonard Smith, Articles Editor
Today's Parents
One Park Avenue
New York, New York 10016

Dear Mr. Smith:

Jennifer Wilson is an eight-year-old charmer with enormous brown eyes, blond pigtails and a fair share of freckles. Like her third-grade classmates, she is learning about American Indians and memorizing her multiplication tables. She's a budding gymnast, and she likes to make clothes for her dolls. To a casual observer, then, Jennifer is a normal little girl. But those close to her know that she is wrestling with one of the gravest traumas a young life can sustain: the recent death of her mother.

Jennifer is not alone. While the loss of a parent is a particularly stressful event, the death of any significant person in a child's life can be traumatic. According to a study done by Elaine Cummings, former co-ordinator of education and training at the St. Francis Center for Thanatology in Washington, D.C., a majority of children under the age of eighteen report having had to come to grips with the untimely loss of a relative, friend, or teacher. Countless more, of course, know the inevitable but nonetheless devastating pain of losing elderly grandparents. Yet for most of us, death is a difficult topic to discuss with anyone, let alone a child. I propose a 3,500-word article aimed at helping people get children through the deaths of those close to them with as few psychological scars as possible.

Four families—including Jennifer's—have agreed to co-operate with interviews for the article. Jennifer's mother died after a long battle with lung cancer. The other three families are those of thirteen-year-old Kevin Stockright, whose revered soccer coach was killed instantly in an automobile accident; ten-year-old Kirsten James, whose younger sister died of leukemia; and fifteen-year-old Lauren Johnson, whose best friend died of muscular dystrophy.

I also plan to interview top experts in the field of death and dying, including Dan Schaefer and Christine Lyons, authors of *How Do We Tell the Children?* (New York: Newmarket Press, 1986); Eric E. Rofes, editor of *The Kids' Book about Death and Dying* (Boston: Little,

Brown, 1985); and Elisabeth Kubler-Ross, author most recently of *Living with Death and Dying* (New York: Macmillan, 1981). I would also try to get in touch with such well-known people as the family of teacher/astronaut Christa McAuliffe.

In addition to the text, I would include a service box listing the names, addresses and telephone numbers of key support organizations across the country, as well as a box listing the best books and pamphlets on the topic.

I'm confident that the proposed article will touch the hearts of all who read it, and more important, fill a real need for information about this sensitive topic.

A stamped, self-addressed envelope is enclosed for your convenience in replying. I look forward to hearing from you.

Cordially,
Martin Jones

I can assure you that if a query like that had landed on my desk during my editing days, I would have given it far more than casual attention, even if it had come from an unknown, unagented and unpublished writer from Appleton, Wisconsin. I imagine that Leonard Smith at *Today's Parents* would, too. So let's see what happens next. . . .

SAMPLE RELEASE FORM

I,_____,
            (name of interviewee)

give permission to_____
                  (name of author or interviewer)

to use all information supplied by me, regarding my
personal and professional life, for the preparation
of (name of article or feature), to be published in
(name of publication).

  I understand that to help protect my anonymity,
(name of publication) may make changes in the
information so released.

Signed_____

Home Address_____

Soc. Sec. #_____

 **4**

Research Comes First

PICTURE A SUN-SPLASHED SPRING Saturday in Appleton, Wisconsin, with a few patches of snow here and there as the only reminders of the rigors of a north country winter. The crocuses and jonquils have poked their purple and gold crowns up through the once-frozen earth, and as you head for the mailbox, you feel a sudden, inexplicable surge of hope. You pull out a sizable bundle of mail and flip through the usual sweepstakes announcements, mail order catalogues, flyers from people wanting to blacktop your driveway or prune your trees, plus newsletters from local political incumbents. There is also an envelope of cents-off coupons, and—wait! The return address on the last envelope is *Today's Parents*, One Park Avenue, New York, New York 10016. Putting the handful of junk mail down, you tear open the *Today's Parents* envelope and find that the articles editor loved your query about helping children deal with the death of someone close. In fact, he would like to see your article in six weeks, on speculation.

Success! Forgetting the pile of junk mail altogether, you sprint back to the house and, fighting the urge to waste time calling friends and relatives with the glad tidings, you march right to your desk and pull out your file for the article. Then the reality of the situation hits you. Six weeks! What now? Can you really do this?

Of course you can. Because your query letter was so well constructed, you're already off to a good start. What you must do now, before you write a single word, is to complete the research that you began when you decided to write the query letter. Remember, though, that when I was explaining how to write a query letter, I directed you only to "give statistics," or approach "a number of real case history families," or "appropriate experts." I haven't yet given you the techniques for accomplishing those goals. First, we need to go back to the beginning, still using our sample article idea about a child who experiences the death of a significant adult, and run through the whole research process.

Naturally, you'll begin by going to the library. Maybe your topic has been treated in the popular press. Most topics have been. And surely psychologists are interested enough in your topic to have compiled some data. Maybe sociologists are, too. How about the Census Bureau? Perhaps there's even a support group, an association of people who help children through the death of family and friends. Your topic may also have been dealt with in the academic press. Then, too, there may be books that cover your topic.

All right. Your first step at the library is to check the *Readers' Guide to Periodical Literature, Books in Print* (New York: R. R. Bowker), and the card catalogue. Also, check to see whether your library has a computerized catalogue. If so, you can type in any subject, title or author and after a brief search, the computer will display on the monitor a list of the relevant holdings in your own and other libraries, so that you can request an inter-library loan if necessary. Usually, there is one computer for books and one for magazines, and the computers will even print out their lists for you.

There are also specialized reference books for such fields as education, science, business and industry, and the arts, and of course your library's microfilm and microfiche collection is invaluable. In addition, you can consult the *New York Times Index*, especially when you're dealing with current events, and you can also use the *Almanac*, the appendices to unabridged dictionaries, and atlases.

Other references you might consult include *Facts on File: Weekly World News Digest with Cumulative Index* (New York: Facts on File, Inc.), the *Social Issues Resources Series* (located in the Young Adult section), and the *En-*

cyclopedia of Associations (Detroit: Gale Research Corporation). This last set has a key word index, and lists contact people, addresses and phone numbers. (That's how I found Elaine Cummings, the "death educator" I referred to in our sample query letter in Chapter 3. I first called the St. Francis Center (202) 363-8500, and I was given Ms. Cummings's home phone number after I explained what kind of information I needed.) And don't forget the telephone books. Libraries have directories from metropolitan areas around the country, and you can find listings for hospitals, government offices, universities, museums, theaters, and even celebrities, many of whom do have listed numbers.

Your next step is to locate your sources, take copious notes, and also check out of the library as many relevant sources as you can. Many, of course, will have to be used in the library, but you can photocopy pages you may want to refer to later. Remember, too much research is far better than not enough, and you can often use the findings from your extra research for future projects. (But if you're a born procrastinator who hates to face that first blank page, or simply a person like me who loves the thrill of the hunt, guard against continuing your research when you ought to be getting started on the writing!)

Back home, search through the books you've taken out, looking for statistics and other information to support your thesis and confirm factual statements. Be sure to write down all bibliographical information, including page numbers, so that the magazine staffers will have no trouble locating or checking your sources and statements later on. (A system of three-by-five cards works especially well here. I buy the kind with holes punched for miniature loose-leaf notebooks so that I can carry them around in my briefcase.)

Now the time has come to contact the associations and experts on your list. If you're not on a tight deadline, you can begin by writing letters, and enclosing stamped, self-addressed envelopes. It's faster, however, to make phone calls. You'll need a tape recorder with a telephone "bug"—an inexpensive little cable with a suction cup on one end to stick onto the receiver, and a plug on the other end to fit into the recorder. (**Important:** When you do an actual interview, be sure to record the interviewee's agreement to allow you to tape the conversation.) Now you're ready to begin calling. You have no idea where to start, but you're hoping that the associations that can't help you directly will be able to lead you to other more appropriate sources, which is frequently the case.

Let's say you start with the American Association of Psychiatric Services for Children, which you found in the *Encyclopedia of Associations*. When the receptionist answers, ask for the public relations or public information department. (If you were calling a department of the United States Government, such as the Department of

Education, you would ask for "public affairs.") A representative from public relations will get on the line. Since you have your go-ahead on speculation, you are free to say that you are "working on an article for *Today's Parents*." Even if a potential interviewee should happen to call to verify your assignment, which oddly enough seldom happens, any staffer at *Today's Parents* would vouch for you after checking with the editor.

A hypothetical conversation might go something like this:

You: Good morning. This is Martin Jones. I'm a writer working on an article for *Today's Parents* magazine on helping children deal with the death of loved ones. I am hoping you'll be able to direct me to the appropriate people in your organization for statistics and interviews on this topic.

PR: Thank you for calling. I'm Bob Walters. Uh, children dealing with the death of loved ones? What magazine did you say?

You: Today's Parents. It's a mass-market magazine aimed at people with both careers and families. The piece I have in mind will be about how to help youngsters cope with the loss of people close to them. Would you have any statistics on this? For example, how many children are touched by this problem? Or would one of your members be especially well versed in this topic and be willing to give me a brief phone interview?

PR: Well, I'm going to have to check my lists. I don't have any names on the tip of my tongue, but I'm sure there are people. What was your name again?

You: Martin Jones. It's best to reach me at my home phone, which is (414) 123-4567. If I'm not available, my answering machine can take the message. Or you might prefer to drop me a note. My address is 123 Some Street, Appleton, Wisconsin 54914.

PR: I'll get right on this and get back to you.

You: Thanks so much. I'm looking forward to hearing from someone soon. Goodbye.

Most often, the PR person will get back to you right away, since his or her job is to disseminate information to the public and make the experts from his organization more visible. If you haven't received a response within a week, you should make a pleasant follow-up call. Maybe the PR person with whom you spoke has been ill, busy, is no longer there, or simply didn't want to bother. You're the one who has to stay on top of getting the names and numbers of the experts who can say what you need them to say.

Now you need real case histories. There are a number of avenues to pursue here. One way is to look for newspaper accounts of people involved in your topic, and write to them. Another is to ask people you know, and that is often surprisingly helpful. You could also contact support groups, and see if any members are willing to talk. Even when you are dealing with a very sensitive issue, I can guarantee that while some people will shy away from exposure, many others will jump at the chance to share their experiences, especially if you agree to conceal their identities. It has been my experience in dealing with delicate emotional areas that for many people, getting the problem out in the open, as a way of helping others in a similar situation, is actually gratifying.

You could also call or write to the public relations departments of hospices, hospitals, non-profit family service counseling agencies, and private counseling and psychiatric services, as well as school guidance counselors. While it is true that health care professionals guarantee that their clients' cases will always be kept confidential, some professionals will in fact privately ask clients if they would consider being interviewed as long as a release form*, which states that identities will be concealed, is signed. If the clients are interested, the counselor or therapist will usually give the clients your number, rather than the other way around. This way, the clients initiate the contact, and no breach of confidentiality is involved. I'm not saying this is an easy way to get interviews, but with persistence it can be done.

But what about getting those coveted interviews with celebrities? Naturally, a go-ahead from a recognized publication helps a lot. Editors who deal at all with celebrities have a great many stellar names on their Rolodexes, and in addition they are very likely registered with Celebrity Service, an organization that publishes the *Celebrity Register*, a constantly updated record of the comings and goings of a long list of luminaries.

As a beginning writer, however, you will prob-

*See form at end of Chapter 3.

ably be on your own. In the public library, you'll
find Michael Levine's *The New Address Book:
How to Reach Anyone Who's Anyone* (New York:
Putnam, 1986), as well as *Who's Who in America*,
and all of its offshoots, such as *Who's Who in the
East*, and other parts of the country. Also, depending on who your celebrity is, you can try
calling relevant trade organizations, college
alumni associations, places of employment, book
publishers, television stations, even television or
radio talk shows on which your celebrity has
been a guest, or newspapers and magazines that
have carried stories about the famous person.
(Check the *New York Times Index* and *The Readers' Guide to Periodical Literature*.) In many
cases, you will reach a receptionist who will chant
the standard (and accurate), "I'm sorry, but we
are not authorized to give out telephone numbers." Don't give up. Quickly and politely ask the
receptionist if you could leave your name, number,
and a brief message, which will then be forwarded
to the celebrity, or failing that, if you could address a letter to the celebrity in care of the organization or publication, which the receptionist
would then forward.

In addition, you may be surprised to find that
the phone numbers of many notable people are
actually listed—look in the phone book or dial
information, and try your luck. And finally, keep
track of dates and times when certain celebrities

are scheduled to speak or give a concert in or near your hometown, and try for an interview then.

You've taken notes from your secondary sources (books, magazines, newspapers) and you've gone as far as collecting a sheaf of phone numbers for your primary sources (experts, as well as "real people," as editors tend to call the ordinary folks you'll use for many anecdotes, and celebrities). Now, take a deep breath and get ready for the true challenge—obtaining the interviews, and conducting them successfully. Onward, then, to the techniques that will get you the facts and quotes you need to make your articles stand out from the rest.

5

How to Conduct Interviews

THERE ARE THREE WAYS to interview people: in person, on the phone, and by mail. The most desirable, of course, is the in-person interview, since in addition to getting responses word for word on tape, you can read your subject's facial expressions and body language, observe physical characteristics, clothes, and surroundings, and use your own expressions and gestures to connect with the person and get him to open up to you. I would say that as a rule of thumb, if the interview is the crux of your story—that is, if you are writing a whole article about someone's personal tragedy, or if you are doing a celebrity profile—the face-to-face interview is essential.

I do all of my "Can This Marriage Be Saved?" interviews in person, for example, usually right in the couples' homes so that I can get a firsthand view of their lifestyle. In this particular feature, as is often true for case history people in other articles concerning personal issues, the names and other details are changed to conceal identities, but the essence of the individuals and the flavor of their speech, if not the exact wording, are preserved. I always have my subjects sign a release form, and ask them to agree on tape to be interviewed. At the beginning of each interview, I simply include the following interchange: *Writer:* May I tape-record what we have to say? *Interviewee:* Yes. And I do allow interviewees to see the final edited galleys just before we go to press. This gives them about forty-eight hours to suggest minor changes, and I try to offer the courtesy of complying if the requests are minimal and reasonable. However, the signed release form really does give me the final say as to what will be printed. Also, as I've mentioned earlier, many magazines (especially the major national ones) employ a libel lawyer who reads all manuscripts and determines whether or not the material could possibly provoke a suit.

There are times, certainly, when release forms are not necessary and a phone interview is sufficient. When you are doing a reportage piece—a written account of collected research, news, insights, and personal experiences, such as the one about helping children deal with the death of loved ones—you'd never meet your deadline if you had to traipse all over the country seeing experts in person. Usually, if you're well prepared with questions, you can get the quotes you need in fifteen to twenty minutes on the phone. I accomplish this by doing a great deal of research *before* calling the expert, then writing what I suspect or hope his responses will be, and only then rephrasing the statements as questions. For example, I might come up with a statement such as, "A young child tends to blame himself irrationally for the death of a loved one, feeling that by being 'bad,' or once wishing the person were hurt or killed, he was responsible for the tragedy." Then I would pose the question to the expert in this way: "I understand that very young children are quite self-centered and may personalize the loss of a loved one. Is this so, and in what way?" Bingo! The expert gives me precisely the quote I need. You can also do your case history interviews on the phone in a similar way, but you'll get more color and depth in person, even for a one-paragraph anecdote.

Interviews by mail, frankly, are a last resort. For any interview, you must prepare a list of questions ahead of time, but in a mail interview, you cannot adjust your questions as you hear and react to the person's responses. By mail, you also forgo the chance to ask experts to define terms or go into more detail on a complicated topic, and you never get the flavor of the interviewee's speech. Still, an interview by mail is better than nothing, and in the case of important people who are loath to speak extemporaneously to a reporter, you will have to settle for the written

interchange. Even so, if the expert is connected
with an institution or corporation, I would try one
last compromise before giving up on a phone interview completely. Ask the PR person or agent
or whoever is handling the press whether you
could send a list of questions for Mr. Newsmaker
to peruse before the phone interview. Often the
celebrity will feel safer seeing in advance the
questions you plan to ask, and then once you have
him on the phone, you can coax him to ramble
from the set questions.

How do you get him to do that? That's part of
your interviewer's bag of tricks. But let's not get
ahead of ourselves. First, as I pointed out earlier,
you need a portable tape recorder, plus a phone
bug. Being the nervous type, I actually use two
tape recorders, especially when I am doing an
exclusive interview with someone hard to reach.
Also, before beginning any interview, make sure
you have an adequate supply of batteries and
blank tapes. Mark each side of each tape either
just before you begin speaking, or immediately
after the tape is removed from the recorder, even
if you have to interrupt the interview briefly. And
devise some kind of tape filing system so that you
don't have to rummage through a drawerful of
cassettes every time you want a certain tape.

In addition to the tape recorder, I also recommend a stenographer's notebook and a clutch of
sharp pencils when you're interviewing in person.
But why take notes at all, when you'll have a

complete recording of the interview? For one thing, I find that writing down key points during an in-person interview keeps you alert and for some reason flatters the interviewee, especially if you nod, smile, and make approving noises while jotting, indicating that you are really *listening*, not merely recording. Second, you can stop whenever necessary and ask for addresses, phone numbers, titles, ages, exact spellings of names, and other facts that might be hard to hear clearly on the tape. Third, in a person-to-person interview you'll want to observe and write down visual details and expressions. Finally, the good old-fashioned reporter's notebook is your insurance against the unthinkable—the simultaneous failure of your tape recorders.

But enough about the tools. Now for the techniques, such as how to get Mr. Newsmaker to speak freely when he hadn't wanted to talk at all; how to get Dr. Expert to translate the jargon of his specialty into plain English; and how to get Mrs. Ordinary to express the depths of her grief or the height of her joy.

Let's start with Mrs. Ordinary, since much of what I have to say about dealing with her applies to the others as well. First and most important, remember that you are not having a conversation. You are trying to get your subject to talk and talk and talk—often about extremely painful topics. The minute you break in with "Oh, I know just how you feel! Why, when my Aunt Ida had a gall bladder attack, we . . ." you've lost the thread of the interview. Yes, you can make little comments now and then, but your main job is to nod sympathetically and say such things as, "That's fascinating! What happened next?" or "Really? Oh, please go on." You must be sincere, so that your subjects trust you and open up to you, and you must also nudge them, keep them on track with brief but pertinent questions such as, "You drove your child to the hospital by yourself when the volunteer ambulance broke down? Goodness! How far away was the hospital, and was there anybody with you?"

That's how you get the facts that keep the story straight. But you must also get the emotional tone and details by asking such questions as, "When you were alone in that car with such a desperately ill child, what thoughts were running through your mind?" Or "As a parent myself, I can't imagine how you could have stayed in control enough to drive! How did you ever do it?" And don't forget to try for the less-than-noble emotions that make the interviewee less saintly, more accessible, by saying such things as, "During the months that the baby was throwing up three times a night, did you ever lose patience?"

In the meantime, of course, you are making note of visual details—the color of everybody's eyes, the fabric on the living room chairs, the breed of dog owned by the stricken family. Note also those telling, emotional gestures—"Strokes baby's head," "Smiles wistfully, stares out window," "Leafs through photo album," "Brushes back a stray lock of hair."

These techniques, by the way, are just as effective with celebrities as they are with ordinary people. In fact, if anything, it's easier to get celebrities to talk easily because many of them are terribly interested in themselves, and they are often also interested in publicity. If you can present yourself as a sincere person who is fascinated by their stories and opinions, they'll favor you with more quotes than you could have dreamed of. It is also a good idea, however, to do your homework first—visit the library and bone up as much as possible on the celebrity's life and work, and if possible, for a major story, call a clipping service. That way, when Rita Rockstar mentions the first time she saw New York City, you'll be able to say something like, "Oh, right, you're from St. Louis, aren't you?" Celebrities—all people, actually—love knowing that the writer has taken pains to be knowledgeable about them, and they'll really warm up to you. One celebrity even complimented me on my wit and intelligence at the end of an interview during which I had said practically nothing. But of course what I *had* said had been about her. . . .

Also, whether you are dealing with celebrities or ordinary people, you must learn how to broach personal topics. I once did a celebrity round-up for *Town & Country* about the lifestyles of several prominent women. The editor wanted me to include information about the interviewees' health habits, but in my first submission, I left out any mention of smoking or alcohol use. I just couldn't figure out how to say to an interviewee like Phyllis George, "Do you drink?" Naturally, I didn't get away with the omission. The editor sent me right back to my telephone for another round of interviews. It turned out that asking "Do you drink?" or "Do you smoke?" was exactly what I had to do and the celebrities were neither surprised nor offended—in fact, they rather enjoyed answering me.

Since then, I've gotten so used to asking personal questions that I can quiz celebrities and ordinary people alike about anything from drug abuse to adultery to compulsive gambling without drawing a nervous breath. The secret is to be genuinely interested, calm, and sympathetic. And again, don't let the interview turn into a conversation. Suppose an interviewee says, "And then I tried a little cocaine, and it made me feel so powerful. With all the strain I was under, dealing with Michael's affair and the twins' mental illness, I guess I just couldn't resist escaping into the white powder. I don't know. Wouldn't you have done the same thing?" You have to keep your expression neutral, think fast, and lob the ball right back to her, saying something like, "I've never been in a situation quite that stressful. You really had a lot on your plate. It must have been hard to handle. Tell me more about how you felt during that time."

When it comes to interviewing the experts, however, you don't have to worry so much about avoiding the conversation format as you do about respectfully forcing them to speak in English, not in technical language. If a doctor says "pulmonary squamous cell carcinoma," stop him until he has translated that into "terminal lung cancer." Again, you should do some preliminary research of your own, checking *Merck's Manual* and the *Physicians' Desk Reference* if you're interviewing a medical specialist, or whatever sources are relevant to the specific field you're writing about, so that you will know which questions to ask and which avenues to pursue.

When dealing with experts, or even in some cases with celebrities or ordinary people, you must also learn when and when not to be somewhat adversarial. That is, if someone expresses an opinion that is shocking or controversial, do you keep a bland but interested look on your face (or tone in your voice over the phone), or do you challenge the assertion? Only you can decide which ploy will result in the most information and the best quotes for any given article. As a case in point, I was doing a grueling job of research not long ago for a piece on parents' roles in the rise in "youth disorder"—teen suicide, drug abuse, teen pregnancy, and so on. Not surprisingly, the topic of working mothers came up over and over, whether I was talking with psychologists, mothers, teen-agers, educators, or sociologists. When it came to male experts who were blatantly opposed to working mothers, especially mothers who had "latch-key kids," I found that the bland-but-interested technique kept them talking. I'm a working woman, after all, and they had no way of knowing whether they would be stepping on my toes by denouncing certain aspects of a working mother's lifestyle. Consequently, I stayed as neutral and professional as possible, making it clear that I was not judging their opinions, but simply recording them for use in the context of my article.

On the other hand, I found that I had to needle the "real people," both the parents and the children, in order to get the most honest quotes. I was getting a lot of platitudes about "quality time" until I pulled out all the stops and did my Phil Donahue/Mike Wallace number on my hapless subjects. ("Come on! Do you mean to tell me that when you come dragging in the door at 6:30 p.m. after a terrible day at the office and a bumper-to-bumper commute, you're ready for 'quality time' with your kids?")

But whether you are respectful or purposely provocative, you need to know how to end an interview. When you have heard all you really need to hear, say something like, "This has been extremely helpful, and I can't tell you how grateful I am to you for having given your time." Often at this moment, especially if you turn off your tape recorder as though preparing to leave, something wonderful will happen. The absolutely best quote of the day will pop out of your subject's mouth.

Eventually, of course, even the last magic moment ends, and you do finish. It won't be difficult to thank your subject profusely but sincerely, since the interview process is an amazingly intimate one in which you become extremely close to people in a very short time. In fact, getting to know the strengths and weaknesses, the joys and sorrows, as well as the impressive expertise and accomplishments of so many fellow human beings is one of the high points of this very special and revealing kind of writing. During the week or so following your research time, while you're still feeling strongly about your interviewees, drop them each a thank-you note, and get a note off to each agent or contact person as well. You want to be remembered as someone they'll all trust and enjoy working with again and again.

Now, you've got three-by-five cards crammed with information from your secondary sources. You've got interviews on tape from experts, ordinary people, and celebrities, and you're all set to transcribe them. About three weeks have gone by since the morning you first pulled that go-ahead letter out of the mailbox. The crocuses and jonquils have given way to roses. The limbs of the maple and oak trees are swelling with new leaves. It's time to resist the call of the out-of-doors and buckle down to a fortnight of the hardest but the most gratifying work of your life.

Turn the page. We're ready to write!

6

Start With Structure

GOOD WRITING IS A COMBINATION of talent and skill—and persistence. If you genuinely love language, take pleasure in reading, and delight in turning a phrase, you probably have the talent. Most born writers confess that they write in their heads almost all the time, wording and rewording, mentally turning a lovely landscape into a descriptive passage or making overheard snatches of conversation into dialogue, almost without being able to help themselves. But of course for a writer—just as for a baseball player or a ballet dancer or a musician—simply being a natural is not enough. You must harness your talent by learning the difficult craft of putting words on paper so that they get your points across clearly. To help you do this, I'm going to explain how to create a solid basic structure for your articles in general, and then in subsequent chapters, I'll give examples of how to flesh out your pieces.

TOPIC SENTENCE

Your first step is to write a one-sentence précis of your article. This summary, which is for your eyes only, forces you to focus your piece and to be certain that all the elements will be included. Here are some examples:

Working Title: "Greenhouse Gardening Made Simple"

Topic Sentence: This how-to article, intended for a novice, will cover types of greenhouses (free-standing, lean-to, solar); costs, choosing the site; building permits; kits vs. custom-built; tools and materials; footings and foundations; special problems in certain climates; heating systems, vents, blinds, and power failure alarms; plant care; pest control; and a greenhouse calendar.

Working Title: "Teen Suicide: A Hard Look at a National Tragedy"

This investigative piece will include case histories, theories from experts on why the problem is so widespread, statistics on the rise of teen suicide, a sidebar listing signs of teen-age depression, a sidebar listing hotlines and other sources of help, and a wrap-up with specific suggestions for dealing with the situation.

Working Title: "I Was Fired"

This personal experience piece, by a middle-aged family man who lost his job after twenty years with the same company, shares his emotional reactions and tells how he managed to tell his family and friends, how he proceeded to pick up the pieces of his life, how he survived financially, and how he finally found a new job that paid less but satisfied him more.

OUTLINE

Once you have your topic sentence, you're ready to create an outline, one that includes your "lead," takes you step-by-step through all of your points, and finishes with a "wrap-up." I'll give you the outline format here, using the greenhouse story as an example, and then in Chapter 8, when we actually go into the process of writing a magazine article, I'll give you an example of a complete outline.

Greenhouse Gardening Made Simple

  I. *Lead:* If you've always wanted a greenhouse, you'll be pleasantly surprised at how easy and affordable one can be.

 II. *Types of greenhouses*

   A. Free-standing

     1. pros and cons

     2. costs

       a. custom-built

       b. kits

   B. Lean-to's

     1. pros and cons

     2. costs

       a. custom-built

       b. kits

C. Solar
  1. pros and cons
  2. costs
    a. custom-built
    b. kits

Using that basic format, you would go on to list all your points, and then indicate a wrap-up. Producing a good outline is somewhat tedious, but I would suggest working and reworking it so that you get the kinks out of your structure *before* you begin writing.

LEADS

There are several types of leads, but all share one feature: they are attention-grabbing, making the reader want to stay with the piece instead of turning the page. For the greenhouse story, a how-to piece, we could use the second person, or "you" approach, immediately addressing the reader himself and drawing him into the subject:

> Imagine orchids at Christmastime, violets in February, plus brilliant displays of asters, campanulas, marigolds, and morning glories. . . . Picture prize-winning tomatoes, and think about having fresh crops of herbs all year 'round. As a greenhouse gardener, you can enjoy these riches and many more—and a greenhouse is easier to build and more affordable than you think. Follow along for our complete guide to hothouse horticulture.

A second approach would be to start with an anecdote:

Jim Swenson and his wife, Margaret, are the proud owners of an impressive free-standing fiberglass greenhouse. Even more impressive, they built the structure themselves, using one of the kits now on the market.

"We considered a custom-built model, but the cost was more than we could handle," says Jim, 42, a certified public accountant. "Actually, building the greenhouse was a lot of fun, and now we spend almost all our leisure time working in it."

The Swensons specialize in starting vegetables and annuals for planting in the spring, but they also enjoy experimenting with orchids and other exotic blooms. If you'd like to share the Swensons' passion for hothouse horticulture, read on for a complete guide to this popular pastime.

A third possibility is to start with facts and figures, if they are arresting enough, and a fourth is to think up some amalgamation of the choices I've given. Just be sure that what you write will hook your potential readers into the story—not put them to sleep!

TRANSITIONS

Never underestimate the magic of well-written transitions. I like to think of transitions as stepping stones. They link the sections of your article, getting you safely from one thought to the next, but they are a little slippery and precarious. You must be both daring and watchful when you're using them, but therein lies the vitality of these deceptively simple sentences that make the difference between an amateurish and a professional article. In fact, if every working writer would learn the art of creating transitions, magazine line editors would practically be out of work, since so much of their time is spent putting transitions into writers' pieces.

Suppose you are writing that article on helping a child deal with the untimely death of a family member or friend. Your introduction finishes with the sentence, "Ironically, death has continued to be a sensitive topic, even as the proliferation of violent movies and television programs has tended to desensitize all of us to the reality of the loss of human life." This being the case, how are we going to make the transition to the next paragraph—coming to terms with *our own* feelings and helping children understand the concept of death? You might be tempted to skip the whole problem and start the next paragraph as though nothing whatsoever had preceded it. For example:

> You cannot hope to help a child understand and deal with death until you have faced your own feelings about mortality.

There's nothing wrong with that sentence *per se* and it's even quite a nice thesis sentence for the paragraph to follow. But it does not make the transition from one thought to another. Here's a better transition:

> These disturbing trends, however, only heighten the importance of addressing rather than avoiding an individual child's emotional needs when a significant person in his or her life dies. The trouble is, you can't do that

effectively until you have come to terms with your own feelings about mortality.

Transitions are vital in every type of magazine article, from how-to to personal experience, from investigative reporting to humorous anecdotes. A well-written outline should help you with transitions, but be sure to check every manuscript before submitting to make sure you've managed to move sensibly and smoothly from section to section.

WRAP-UPS

When you've said all that you have to say, don't just leave your article open-ended. Write a brief summary of the piece, one that amounts to a little refresher course on the points you've made, or a recapitulation of the philosophy you've tried to present in a human interest or think piece. For the greenhouse article:

> As you can see, joining the ranks of greenhouse gardeners is not as complicated or expensive as you might have thought. Just choose your sites and materials with care, decide on the best type of greenhouse for you, and follow the calendar for the finest in blooms and vegetables. The best of luck as you begin this rewarding adventure!

For the article on helping children deal with death:

> Yes, the untimely death of a friend or family member is one of life's most unbearable tragedies, yet for children

like Jennifer, whose mother died of cancer, and for Kevin, whose beloved soccer coach was killed in a car accident, the grief *can* be overcome as long as those close to the youngsters go about helping them face the facts and bear the pain. When that happens, the children can grow into emotionally healthy adults, becoming even stronger for having survived the suffering.

With a solid structure in place, it's time to write with all the clarity and precision you can muster. Our next stop, therefore, is a discussion of grammar and style. . . .

7

How Do You Say It Right?
Language and Style

N O MATTER HOW GIFTED you may be, you can't become a selling writer if you haven't learned the rules of English grammar. From my own observation during years of reading queries and manuscripts, a great many people in this country, ranging from those who have dropped out of school to those with graduate degrees, continue to butcher our mother tongue. I won't venture to guess where the fault lies, but I would advise you to be honest about your own mastery of the language, and to take brush-up college or continuing education courses if you feel you need them.

In the meantime, I'll give you examples of the three types of garbled sentences that editors see far too often:

GRAMMAR

● **Dangling participle**
Wrong: "Wearing gardening gloves, the tools and soil won't damage your hands."
(This would mean that the tools and soil were wearing the gardening gloves!)
Right: "If you wear gardening gloves, the tools and soil won't damage your hands."

● **Number disagreement**
Wrong: "A child under the age of three is often frightened when they are separated from their parents."
(This is called "number disagreement" because the noun is singular and the pronouns plural.)
Right: "Children under the age of three are often frightened when they are separated from their parents." OR
"A child under the age of three may be frightened when she is separated from her parents."

● **Pronoun with no clear antecedent**
Wrong: "Steven stood absolutely still as the bear approached slowly. He was dirty and tired and very hungry."
("He" technically refers to the bear, not to Steven, but we can't be sure from the context what the author meant.)
Right: "Steven stood absolutely still while the

bear approached slowly. The little boy was dirty and tired and hungry." OR

"Steven stood absolutely still while the bear approached slowly. The huge animal was dirty and tired and hungry."

STYLE

Beyond grammar—beyond words that are properly spelled, sentences that are accurately formed, paragraphs that have a beginning, middle, and end—lies the more nebulous subject of style. Grammar and style overlap at times, certainly, but the latter has less to do with what is correct and what is incorrect, and more to do with what lifts a piece of prose out of the ordinary and into the realm of fine writing. The best advice I can give you here is to read and reread a slim but invaluable volume, *The Elements of Style*, by William Strunk, Jr. and E.B. White (3rd Ed. New York: Macmillan, 1979). More than just a rule book, this concise classic is a paean to eloquence, one that no serious writer can afford to be without. Keep it at hand for ready reference and checking.

Here's a quick refresher on the basics of style:

● **Vary sentence structure and length**

Nothing is more boring than a piece in which almost every sentence is subject-verb-object, with about the same number of words.

Bad: "Greenhouse gardening is an interesting hobby. The whole family can get involved. Many flowers and vegetables thrive in greenhouses. You can build your own greenhouse. A greenhouse is not very expensive."

Better (and more informative): "Greenhouse gardening, the indoor sport of horticultural enthusiasts, can be a rewarding hobby for the whole family. Why? You can cultivate Cape primroses, coleuses, snapdragons and petunias, cloister your holiday poinsettias, give vegetable seedlings a gentle start, nurture softwood cuttings from begonias, geraniums, and fuchsia. And that's just the beginning! What's more, with one of the kits now available, you can build your own customized hothouse for far less than you'd imagine."

- **Don't repeat key words too often**

Bad: "Greenhouse gardening is an interesting hobby. The whole family can get involved. Many flowers and vegetables thrive in greenhouses. You can build your own greenhouse. A greenhouse is not very expensive."

Better: "Greenhouse gardening is an interesting hobby that the whole family can enjoy. Many flowers and vegetables thrive in these attractive indoor havens—and you can build your own for less than you'd think, with several styles to choose from."

● **Use adjectives and adverbs, but avoid redundancy and "purple prose"**

Modifiers, those magical words that engage the senses, are what give your prose color, texture, rhythm, flavor, and fragrance. Use them, but use them judiciously and even sparingly, like a sprinkling of a delicate blend of the best spices in a gourmet recipe. Otherwise, adjectives and adverbs strung out one after the other can befuddle the reader, making your points unclear. Too many modifiers will simply cancel each other out, leaving your piece as flat as it would have been without any descriptive words at all—and hard reading in the bargain. In addition, never be guilty of redundancy—using synonyms all in row, when one word was all you needed. Spare writing is the best. Remember, too, that verbs and nouns, when chosen for connotation rather than simple denotation, can be evocative and powerful without any modifiers at all.

Bad: "On the cold, frosty, winter evening of January 16 of last year, the quiet, sleepy, small, unknown hamlet of Cooley Lake, Michigan, was the scene of a rare, unprecedented crime. Stealthily, walking without making a sound, two tall, lanky, angular young men not much more than twenty years old, strolled through the town's main street in the bright, luminous light of a brilliant moon, looking for unsuspecting, unwitting victims."

Better: "On January 16 of last year, the sleepy hamlet of Cooley Lake, Michigan, was the scene of an unprecedented crime. Sometime between midnight and two a.m., walking stealthily so as not to crunch the snow underfoot, two lanky youths prowled the town's main street in the moonlight, hunting down victims."

● Use figures of speech
You know these, of course, but here's a review of the most important ones:

Metaphor: Comparing one thing to another by implying that the two are identical.

"A mighty fortress is our God."

"That woman is a doormat."

"The violets, dear little purple faces all in a row, delighted the child."

Simile: Comparing one thing to another, using "as" or "like."

"He's as strong as an ox."

"She sings like an angel."

"Twinkle, twinkle, little star, like a diamond in the sky."

Personification: Attributing human characteristics and capabilities to abstractions or inanimate objects.

"A gentle breeze caressed her cheek."

"The brilliant sun was the only witness to that noontime murder in a deserted cornfield."

"The idea became an obsession, making her its slave."

Onomatopoeia: Forming or using a word that imitates a sound.

Bleep, beep, boom, swish, cuckoo, screech, thud, thump, splat, tweet, chirp, twitter, whoosh, zoom, rat-a-tat-tat, bark, meow, oink, cackle, bleat, moo, whinny, whine, hee-haw, cock-a-doodle-doo, and so on. You don't want your prose to read like a Marvel comic, but a little of this aural vocabulary here and there can be very effective, if used sparingly. Most often, it is a poor way to characterize.

Alliteration: Using words that repeat the initial consonant sound:

"Fast and ferocious, these wildcats almost always get their prey."

"Looking slim and self-confident after two weeks at a spa, she answered reporters' questions easily."

"The sunset sent shimmering ribbons across the little inland lake."

Antithesis: Placing direct opposites one after another for dramatic effect.

"Give me liberty or give me death."

"Feast or famine"

"All or nothing"

- **Avoid clichés**

Ironically, clichés—overused idioms and figures of speech—have become clichés precisely because they are so good, so expressive. Still, while I've used a few clichés as examples of figures of speech ("She sings like an angel," "feast or famine"), I wouldn't use them in my own writing—with one exception. When I'm writing monologues or dialogues that represent the speech of interviewees, I use the clichés that my interviewees actually use, since this makes the speech patterns ring true. For example, the therapist or counselor may tell me that the wife is "clinically obese," but her complaining husband will tell me that she's gotten herself "fat as a pig" by eating him "out of house and home," and that's exactly what I would choose to print. In other forms of writing, however, I'd strive for fresher phrasing, new ways of wording what I see and think and feel.

• Clarity

If grammar and style are important, clarity is paramount. The best nonfiction writers get information across without fail, but also engage and entertain readers. Less experienced writers either tell too little, or explain their points in a verbose or roundabout manner. "Verbose," by the way, doesn't mean that there are too many words in the whole article, but that there are too many words devoted to a single point or concept, or that some words are extraneous. Entertaining, clear writing may or may not use more words than an obtuse version of the same idea, but the clear version will always be more readable and easier to understand. Here are some examples:

Bad, because too much is left unsaid: "After weeks of waiting, Walter Nastasi couldn't believe the final diagnosis: malignant melanoma."

Bad, because too much is said in one sentence, and yet still not enough is reported: "After finding a lump in his thigh, and submitting to a biopsy, then waiting two weeks for a lab report, Walter Nastasi couldn't believe the final diagnosis of malignant melanoma, a form of skin cancer that almost certainly has already metastasized, or spread, by the time it is detected, and is almost always lethal."

Better: "Soaping himself in the shower one morning, Walter Nastasi, a husky thirty-eight-year-old bricklayer from Hannibal, Missouri, felt a lump on the inside of his left thigh. Two days passed before he got up the courage to call the family doctor. The nurse who answered the phone, alarmed at Nastasi's symptom, scheduled him for an appointment that very afternoon. The doctor recommended a biopsy, and Nastasi knew that this meant the possibility of cancer. He didn't ask questions. He didn't tell his wife and kids. He made up a phony trip to visit a cousin in Kansas, and checked himself into the hospital. Then he waited two weeks for the lab report, telling himself that no news was good news. It wasn't. Nastasi was the victim of malignant melanoma, a form of skin cancer the doctor explained is almost certainly lethal by the time it is palpable—that is, big enough to be detected by hand. But Nastasi still didn't believe his number was up. He made up his mind to fight. And he did."

In the third example, above, Walter Nastasi has become a "sympathetic protagonist," a hero we know and care about, one with whom we can empathize. Creating empathy is another important aspect of effective article writing. Little details such as his age, his occupation, his physical appearance, and his macho attempt to mask his fear and protect his family from the truth have been worked in to make him come alive for the reader. Of course, if you are writing about a serial murderer, you can't make him a sympathetic protagonist, but you *can* make him an object of fascination by probing the possible workings of his sociopathic mind. You can also make his *victims* into sympathetic characters by divulging human interest tidbits—maybe one young woman was planning her wedding, maybe another had just gotten her first job, and so on.

Actually, the lead for Walter Nastasi's ordeal brings us easily into the final technique tip I'd like to mention: the art of storytelling. Many types of nonfiction require you to become a facile spinner of yarns, a writer who understands the elements of good fiction writing and applies them to the true stories you are telling. Creating characters who come alive, as I did with Nastasi, is the first step. Here are the others:

• Plotting

Outline your true stories, just as you would fiction, taking care to weave in a bit of mystery, dropping "plot plants" (hints about what might be going to happen), but keeping the reader in suspense until the end. For example:

I. *Lead:* Walter Nastasi discovers a lump in his thigh.
   A. Goes to doctor, has biopsy
   B. Doesn't tell family and friends
   C. Finds out he has malignant melanoma, lethal cancer

II. Nastasi tells wife and six kids, vows to fight for life.
   A. Wife vows support, gets a job
   B. Kids vow support, older ones get jobs; three-year-old crawls up on Daddy's lap and gives him a kiss and offers his teddy bear

III. Nastasi not accepted in experimental drug program at nearby hospital; doesn't meet test criteria.

IV. Nastasi finally accepted in drug program in another state.

V. Nastasi tells boss, quits job; buddies have a farewell party a local bar where they all watch sports on TV.

VI. Neighbors raise money via bake sales and raffles for Nastasi's plane fare and other expenses.

VII. Nastasi says goodbye to family, flies to hospital, enters program.

VIII. Nastasi undergoes painful treatments, suffers terrible side effects, no results.

IX. Nastasi flies home for rest period, family and friends horrified at his weakened condition; he and

wife have one evening alone, which friends arrange by taking kids for sleep-overs and having
fabulous meal catered in; Nastasi can't eat.

X. Nastasi goes back to hospital for another drug;
seems to help some.

XI. Nastasi goes home for Christmas and also to at-
tend his eldest child's wedding and the three-year-
old's birthday.

XII. Nastasi goes back for third drug; new tumors ap-
pear.

XIII. Nastasi goes home; dies six months later.

XIV. Last scene is the funeral, a gorgeous sunny summer day, with young widow, all the kids, the whole
town; one of Nastasi's buddies delivers the eulogy
to his brave friend in the kind of rough-hewn
speech Nastasi himself used. At least the trials
bought him some time, and he contributed to
knowledge that will save other lives in the future.

● Play on the reader's emotions

When you are interviewing your subjects, stay
alert for human interest details, and ask questions to elicit them if necessary. In the above
outline, there are several moments that reach
deep into the reader's heart—the three-year-old
offering his Daddy the comfort of a teddy bear;
the buddies throwing a party at the old haunt; the
neighbors arranging a special evening for the
Nastasis.

● Dialogue

When you do your interviews, listen for the
rhythm of people's speech and then try to capture
that in your writing. You're not always going to
put things down verbatim, but it's a mistake to

take all the flavor out and turn your subjects into people with perfect grammar who never use clichés. For example, I once had a counselor tell me that the husband had "manic-depressive mood swings." The wife said, "All I know is, he's got a mean streak just like his father." Needless to say, I didn't change a word of that!

Also, it's important to sprinkle dialogue throughout many types of articles:

Bad: "Walter Nastasi gathered his family in the living room after dinner and told them he had cancer, but that he was going to fight the disease in any way possible."

Better: "Walter Nastasi gathered his family in the living room after dinner that evening. A man of few words, he shifted in his seat, searching for a way to say that he had just been handed a death sentence by his doctor. The younger children stared at their father with obvious curiosity. He had never asked them all to sit down together like this before.

"Maureen," Nastasi finally said, addressing his wife and clearing his throat. "Uh, Maureen, kids, I gotta tell you something—something not so great. I been to the doctor. He says I got, uh, cancer. But, hey, don't you guys worry. You know your old man, right? Am I gonna let this get me? Heck, no!"

And with that, your bag of writing tricks is full. It's time to move on to special techniques for special kinds of articles.

 **8**

How to Write A General Article

DID YOU RUN YOUR FINGER down the contents of this book and decide to turn directly to this chapter, skipping all the laborious preliminaries and getting right to the meat of the matter? If so, go back to square one immediately! This chapter and those that follow are based on the assumption that you already know all the basics I've been talking about until now, and you'll only end up with a pile of rejection slips if you try to bypass the hard work that *precedes* the actual writing of a piece of salable nonfiction.

Many would-be scribes assume that writing is just writing—some muse-inspired process strictly between the Author (with a capital "A") and the blank page (or blank computer monitor screen). But by now, you know as well as I do that what goes *before* the actual putting together of words on paper is the hardest part. If you've learned your lessons well, you're primed for the moment when you can make all those three-by-five cards, tape recordings, and tips on technique come together and yield a magazine article you'll be proud of—and one that will fill your editor's needs. So let's get on with the process.

By preparing to write your query letter, you have already defined your article idea for a general information magazine piece. By this I mean articles involving research, on a wide range of topics such as the current world political scene, law, medicine, family relationships, finances, society's problems, and the like. To clarify this concept further, here are some possible titles that might make articles:

SUBJECT	POSSIBLE TITLE
Health	"Headache Handbook: The Truth about America's Most Common Health Complaint"
Marital relationships	"Have You Ever Been Attracted to Another Man?"
Family relationships	"There Is Help for Your Aging Parents"
Personal emotions	"How to Handle Criticism"
Finances	"Yes, You Can Afford to Send the Kids to College"
Society's problems	"Helping Our Hometown's Homeless Population"
Child care	"Why Did Mommy Die?— Helping Children Deal with the Loss of Loved Ones"

Having defined your idea and done your research, you're ready to make an outline. While a basic outline format might serve for any of the titles suggested above, I find that no formula works perfectly for all general information articles. And besides, even the most carefully planned outline sometimes needs to be adjusted as the actual article evolves.

My article on parents' roles in the problem of teen-age tragedies, such as drug abuse and suicide, is an example of that. I had decided to deal first with the big picture—the fact that kids today live in a global "information society" that bombards them with images and ideas about everything from nuclear winter to AIDS to international terrorism. I was then going to move to the immediate world youngsters live in—a society with a teeter-totter economy, in which two-career families are the norm, and in which the crisis in public education has prompted a number of books on the subject

Finally, I planned to focus on what individual parents are doing right and wrong in bringing up the next generation of Americans. Logical, right? Well, I thought so, and even went so far as to spend several days writing a good portion of the piece before I realized that I had the whole thing backwards. Starting with the global picture was confusing and tedious, forcing the reader to wade through a great deal of material before any real point was made—the point being that outside influences notwithstanding, parents still have both the responsibility and the power to provide guidance and control for their children. Somewhat wearily, I scrapped much of what I had written, saved what might still be useful, rewrote my outline and started anew. The resulting piece was one I felt confident about submitting to my editor. Sure enough, she did not ask for any structural changes at all, and I was glad that I had been dogged enough to do the job right, instead of handing in a story that the editor would have had to reorganize for me or send back for me to do over.

This is all by way of saying that an outline is not immutable, but it *is* essential. You simply must begin somewhere and create some kind of a blueprint, even if you end up going back to the drawing board. Here, then, is one way we might structure the piece I've been using all along as a teaching tool:

WHY DID MOMMY DIE?
Helping Children Deal with the Loss of Loved Ones
by Martin Jones

I. Introduction
   A. Lead anecdote about Jennifer, an eight-year-old whose mother has died
   B. Estimates about how many children have to cope with the untimely death of family and friends
   C. Mention of how many other children must cope with the inevitable but still devastating loss of grandparents

   D. Expert quotes about how the proliferation of violent movies and television programs has tended to desensitize all of us to the reality of the loss of human life

II. Helping children understand the concept of death in general
   A. Coming to terms with your own feelings
       1. Religious beliefs, if any
           a. Quotes from clergy
           b. Quotes from real people and/or celebrities
       2. Personal fear of mortality
           a. Quotes from psychologists/psychiatrists
           b. Quotes from hospice experts
   B. Understanding developmental stages of children's concept of death
       1. Very young children
           a. Quotes from experts on early childhood
           b. Real case history
       2. Middle childhood
           a. Quotes from experts on middle childhood
           b. Real case history
       3. Adolescence
           a. Quotes from experts on adolescence
           b. Real case history
   C. Dealing with the two ways children experience the death of loved ones
       1. A long, terminal illness
           a. Expert quotes
           b. Real people quotes
       2. Sudden death, such as from a heart attack or car accident
           a. Expert quotes
           b. Reference to celebrity cases, such as family of Christa McAuliffe

   D. A listing of the "stages of grief" as defined by
      psychiatrists
   E. Dealing with loss of the following:
   (Expert and case history quotes for each, explaining
how children tend to blame themselves for the death, and
how they may react by acting out or shutting themselves
away from the world)

      1. A parent (mention stress charts)
      2. A sibling
      3. A revered adult, such as an uncle or a soccer
         coach
      4. A contemporary, a friend
      5. A grandparent

   F. Final points, each with expert quotes
      1. Should the child attend the funeral?
      2. Signs of real trouble coping—when profes-
         sional help is called for
   G. Conclusion—A tender and supportive paragraph,
      bringing back the case history characters for a
      final bow, showing that even life's most searing
      tragedies can and must be overcome and that we
      must all work through our grief and go on living,
      becoming even stronger for having survived the
      suffering

I can't guarantee that this outline would work,
but I've given it a good deal of thought, and it
does seem quite sound. At the very least, it's well
enough charted to get a person started on the
writing of a magazine article. And short of writing the whole piece for you, I've pretty much done
all I can to show you how to go about turning your
research into a cohesive piece. The rest of it—the
way with words, the style, the personal insights,

the special presentation of your case history people—is up to you. This is the moment at which, if you and I were each to set about actually writing this particular story, our articles would become as different in tone and texture as they would be similar in structure and statistical accuracy. Good writing, after all, is not simply a craft, but an art—and not simply a learned skill, but a gift. Thank goodness for that, or else you and I would soon be replaced by computers!

Even so, there are a few more tips I want to share with you before we move on to the next type of magazine article. First, there are four ways to write the lead for a standard magazine piece, as follows:

1. *One riveting anecdote* about a single case history—such as the Jennifer lead we've been using. Just as a refresher, here it is again:

> Jennifer Wilson is an eight-year-old charmer with enormous brown eyes, blond pigtails and a fair share of freckles. Like her third-grade classmates, she is learning about American Indians and memorizing her multiplication tables. She's a budding gymnast, and she likes to make clothes for her dolls. To a casual observer, then, Jennifer is a normal little girl. But those close to her know that she is wrestling with one of the gravest traumas a young life can sustain: the recent death of her mother.

2. *Three brief summaries of case histories,* to show the scope of what you'll be covering. For example:

• Jennifer Wilson, at the tender age of eight, is a motherless child—one who knows what it's like to lose the most important person in her life to something terrible called cancer.

• Kevin Stockright, a strapping sixteen-year-old, quit the soccer team and let his grades drop after his much admired coach was killed in a car accident.

• Kirsten James, ten years old, once shared a room with her younger sister, Karen. Karen died of leukemia a year ago.

What these youngsters have in common is the devastating loss of someone who, etc. etc.

3. *The facts-and-statistics lead:*

• The vast majority of children under the age of twelve in this country have experienced the untimely loss of a loved one.

• A national survey shows that for a majority of youngsters under the age of eighteen, the number one fear is loss of a parent.

• According to hospice personnel—professionals trained to help families cope with death and dying—the average adult has no idea how to discuss death with anyone, least of all with children.

As these facts and statistics clearly indicate, the topic of helping children deal with the death of those close to them is an important one indeed.

4. *The creative lead.* In other words, sometimes you will be inspired to break the rules.

● You could start with a rhetorical question:

"What do you say to an eight-year-old whose mother is dying?"

● You could start with an anecdote using techniques borrowed from fiction writing:

> The beauty of the April afternoon, alive with buttercups and birdsong, served only to deepen little Jennifer's sorrow. Lagging a few feet behind the other children, not wanting to hear their shouts and peals of laughter, she scuffed her way home from school, blinking defiantly now and then as a tear or two escaped from her enormous brown eyes. How could the rest of the world be happy when the most terrible thing imaginable had happened? Jennifer's mommy had died.

● You can come up with something unusual that I have not thought of, and that will set you apart as an original thinker.

My last piece of advice here (and one that also goes for any form of magazine article) is that you must learn to ask the questions an editor would ask and then answer them *before* you submit your manuscript. That is, finish your article, let it cool for a day or two, then take it out, arm yourself with a good sharp pencil, and look at the piece with a ruthless eye. Make margin notes as you go. (How old is this person? . . . Where does Lucille work? . . . Why did she leave the baby alone in the car? . . . Why did the doctor recommend surgery? . . . What is this disease? Who are the usual victims? Is it curable?) If you can learn to be really hard on yourself and catch all these little omissions *before* your editor has to point them out to you, you will become known to editors as a treasure and you will have more assignments than you can handle. Nice thought, and absolutely true.

Now, on to the specialty genres, beginning with "ordeals" or "true-life dramas."

9

Writing the True-Life Drama

TRUE-LIFE DRAMAS, real-life stories, ordeal stories—no matter what we call them, these articles about the extent of human courage are definitely an important part of a writer's arsenal, especially a new writer. Sometimes written in the first person (see Chapter 10 on personal experience pieces), but most often told by the writer as narrator, these pieces can be pure gold. Not only the major markets, but hundreds and hundreds of smaller magazines have a constant need for this type of piece.

Put aside all the jokes about ambulance-chasing journalism and try to understand that as bizarre as some of the events in these stories may be, they are not meant simply to titillate the side-show hunger in human nature. Rather, they fill one or more of four real needs, depending on whether they have happy or sad endings. Ordeals show that there can sometimes be triumph over tragedy; they call up a sense of "There but for the grace of God go I"; they can serve as a warning, a take-heed; and they can let us be awed and inspired by the scope of human fortitude. Surely, that is worthwhile journalism. Add to that an "informational sidebar"—how to get crisis insurance, support groups to contact, symptoms of a disease, whatever might make your story more of a service to the readers—and you have an impressive nonfiction piece that is not only uplifting but genuinely helpful to millions of people. That is something you can be genuinely proud of. Also remember that ordeals are one of the surest ways to break into article writing, simply because your local newspapers are rich sources of stories that editors have no way of knowing about until you present them in your query. And because editors know that these real-life dramas are frequently the best-read pieces in any given issue of their magazines, they are going to be willing to take a chance on a new writer who proposes an irresistible piece.

O.K.—but when you're perusing the newspaper, how can you ascertain whether an incident really qualifies as "ordeal" material? First, rule out everything that is fairly common, no matter how bittersweet, poignant, or courageous. If your true-life drama is a killer disease such as cancer or AIDS, a drunk driving accident, a house on fire, a child with birth defects, or any other common disaster, you need to find an angle, a reason that makes it special. Maybe the cancer victim is a stellar high school athlete in danger of losing one of his legs; or the AIDS victim is a pregnant woman who was infected via a blood transfusion; or the DWI (Driving While Intoxicated) accident victims were newlyweds who had left the church only minutes before; or the burning house trapped an elderly gentleman on the eve of his well-deserved retirement; or the Down's syndrome baby was born to a surrogate mother, stirring up all kinds of emotional and legal problems.

Of course, if you can come up with a "first," so much the better. I've edited some wonderful pieces on the first heart-lung transplant, the first test-tube baby born of American parents, the first children treated with man-made growth hormones, and so on. On the horizon, we might find the first AIDS case to go into remission; the first human fetus brought to term in an artificial womb; the first people to live in a space colony. And then there are the truth-is-stranger-than-fiction stories—like Linda Wolfe's *LHJ* piece "A Tale of Two Mothers," in which an adopted son, when a grown man, falls ill with a liver disease, necessitating the search for his birth mother in order to ascertain whether he has the hereditary form of the disease that would require special treatment. His mother turns out to be living right in his own home town and is someone he knows.

All right—you know what makes a good story. Suppose you've found one. You already know that as a new writer you need to show what you can do by writing an attention-grabbing query letter. Is there anything special about writing an "ordeal" query? Yes. While you might want to include a newspaper clipping or two, plus a couple of sentences about how this might make a good article, you also need to get in touch with the people involved in the ordeal and try to persuade them to give you their story. You should try to offer the editor what is called an "exclusive" magazine story, too. That is, you should attempt to get the subjects to agree not to talk to any other writer preparing a magazine article about them until after your article is published. This is not absolutely essential, but it definitely enhances your chances of getting an assignment, because an exclusive means that two competing magazines won't end up publishing in the same month pieces on the same medical miracle by different writers who interviewed the same person. Editors sometimes, but not always, pay honorariums to the subjects of ordeals stories in order to get exclusives. The fee is usually small—in the neighborhood of one or two hundred dollars—but it might go much higher for a real blockbuster that has never been written about, even in a newspaper. By the way, be sure to get your exclusive agreement in writing.

In addition, if you can take good pictures, you can offer photographs along with your story, although a major magazine will probably want to send a photographer from its own stable. You might also contact the newspaper that covered the story to see whether photographs are available.

Now—the editor gets your sparkling, professional query letter, and you get the go-ahead. The next step is doing the interviews. (Go back to Chapter 5 if you feel you need a refresher on interview techniques.) For illustrative purposes, let's say you're writing the piece mentioned earlier about a stray dog curling around a lost toddler on Christmas Eve, saving the child from death by hypothermia. First you must talk with the parents. I would suggest trying to get separate interviews, first with the mother and then with the father. Later, you might bring the parents together briefly. I've learned from experience that women tend to be more talkative and emotional than men, and in a joint interview, the wife often dominates the conversation so that you get very few quotes from the husband. Also, when the husband is talking with you in private, he is more likely to drop his macho shield, and let you know how he really feels.

While you're talking with the parents, try to learn who the other significant "players" in the drama really are. Were the grandparents or any other relatives involved in any way? Is there a clergyman you should talk with? A baby sitter, perhaps? Neighbors? Was there a particular doctor who performed wonders for the child, and was sympathetic, too? Who found the freezing child?

A policeman? A bag lady? A pair of midnight revelers? Of course, you also need to find out what happened to the dog. Maybe the toddler's family "adopted" him after local TV coverage failed to turn up the owners, or maybe the owners happened to be rich philanthropists who decided to give a million dollars to the local ASPCA in the hero pooch's name. The point is to keep digging. You never know what kind of subplots you're going to unearth. As always, you're better off with too much information rather than too little.

Eventually, though, you'll reach a point where you have to stop digging and move on to doing the rest of your interviews. Try to get quotes from as many of the "characters" as possible. And even though the child is too young to say much, arrange a session where you can observe the happily reunited family.

After that, you'll need to do some library research, boning up on hypothermia, perhaps finding out something about this particular breed of dog, and learning such facts as the population and a brief history of the town. (Check with the Chamber of Commerce, local newspaper, and Town Clerk.) Also, research your sidebar, if any. In this case, you could write about the dangers and aftereffects of hypothermia, or you could write a safety checklist for keeping toddlers from straying, especially during the busy holiday season, whether in shopping malls or at crowded family get-togethers. Next, transcribe your interviews, organize your notes, and make an outline tracking the sequence of events.

Finally, you're ready to write, and you need a lead anecdote, preferably full of suspense, something that hints at what is to come. As you may have gathered by now, from all of my references to "plot plants," "subplots," and "characters," writing an ordeal story is not unlike writing a piece of fiction. With fiction, naturally, you are making the whole thing up, and you are also expressing some point of view or message, some unique way of looking at the world. With the ordeal story, you're simply crafting a compelling version of something that really happened. Still, the actual storytelling process is very similar. So begin with a lead anecdote that gathers your readers in, intrigues them, and makes them want to keep going to find out what happened—something like:

> By 6 p.m. on a frosty Christmas eve, three generations plus assorted aunts and uncles had gathered in the home of Bob and Carol Williams of Charleroi, Pennsylvania, for a festive family get-together. The mood was particularly merry, because Bob and Carol, both 43 years old, were the proud parents of Timmy, their fourth child, born fifteen years after his next oldest sibling. At eleven months, the chubby little towhead was already toddling, and his parents were cherishing every minute of his wide-eyed reactions to the twinkling Christmas tree and the pile of gaily wrapped presents beneath it.
>
> Carol's pregnancy had been something of a surprise, to

be sure, but both Bob and Carol had welcomed this precious new life with all their hearts, and found that he was affording them a special kind of joy they had not quite been mature enough to appreciate when they were bringing up the earlier brood. So it was with special care and anticipation that they had prepared for this holiday gathering when they could let the rest of their close-knit family in on the thrill of sharing a child's first Christmas. Yet their joy was to be short-lived as a bizarre series of events turned this happy evening into a nightmare they would never forget—one that would change their lives, and Timmy's, forever . . . .

Notice that the "who, what, when, why and where" elements of good reporting have been worked into this lead, just as they would be in any newspaper article on the same event. What have been added are the color and emotion that will make the piece a "good read," worthy of 3,500 words in a magazine. We're off to a fine start, and we need to keep it up with plot plants and subsequent revelations that build suspense throughout the piece. There must also be lots of quotes that reflect the real rhythm of the interviewees' speech. Make the people come alive. Make the readers care about them. Also, don't forget about transitions and margin questions to ask yourself before submitting the piece. Then finish with a resonant wrap-up that underscores the four reasons mentioned at the beginning of this chapter that true-life dramas are so appealing to readers. Don't be afraid to use touching details that will make the readers—and the editors—cry. This is human interest writing, and if you can get a veteran editor to shed a few tears, even if she's just getting to your manuscript after closing time on a summer Friday when she'd rather be heading out for the weekend, you've made a sale!

☰ 10

Putting Personal
Experiences
on Paper

THERE ARE TWO KINDS of personal experience
pieces. The first is a cousin of the true-life
drama just discussed, and the second is the opinion essay, usually structured around a life event.
Let's tackle them one at a time.

Unless you've gone through a bona fide "ordeal"—a truly unique dramatic experience or
event—you probably have not had a personal experience worthy of a 3,000-word major magazine
true-life drama article. Even so, it's a good bet
that many of the happenings in your life will provide the material for somewhat shorter pieces.
Happily, the market for these inspirational human
interest articles is vast, with hundreds of publications welcoming beginning and part-time writers
of these pieces. While the pay is often modest, the
pieces are relatively easy to write, since you have
all the information and need not spend time on
research and interviews. This is the kind of article

in which you can tell about your mugging, your cosmetic surgery, your bankruptcy, your aging parents, or your return to college at the age of forty. In other words, this is your chance to tell a story that was personally very important to you, but is not front page news. Check *The Writer's Handbook*, the *Standard Periodical Directory*, as well as the special market lists in *The Writer Magazine*, to discover outlets for this type of piece. The religious magazines gobble them up, most women's magazines have special sections for them, and magazines for men, young adults, and children use them, too. Don't forget the Sunday magazines, and newspapers in general. Specialty magazines—those on food, crafts, travel, media, and the arts—also publish personal experiences. Remember, though, that even with these shorter pieces, you need to take a step back and decide whether your story is worth telling at all. And nowhere is the eloquence and power of your writing more important than in these slice-of-life vignettes. You must be able to transform a fairly ordinary experience into something extraordinary because of the way you observe every detail, express every passion, and make your readers see the world a little differently because of what you've shared with them. One excellent example of a writer's having achieved this goal is a piece entitled "Kiss Daddy Good-Bye," by Peter Mc-Cabe (published in *LHJ*), which tells the all-too-familiar story of a divorced father with limited visitation rights. The writing was sparse but straight from the heart, and I believe that many readers truly felt the sadness in this situation for the first time.

But of course, in personal experience pieces, craft is just as important as art. Because the pieces are so short (not more than five manuscript pages), there is no room for meandering. Dialogue is limited, and your own voice must supply the authenticity that dialogue provides in longer ordeal pieces. You must strip away everything expendable until you have found the kernel of your story, and yet you must not alter the facts or the sequence of events. This is a very difficult task, particularly since you are writing in the first person and must fight to remain objective about what is and is not essential to the telling of the tale. On the other hand, you must understand that complete emotional disclosure is the appeal of these pieces, because your honesty is what evokes strong reader identification with your experience. You must be willing to divulge your innermost thoughts, letting the readers in on the private workings of your heart and mind. A writer can spend more time anguishing over letting the world in on secret doubts and dreams than on actually writing the piece. What can help get you over the hurdle is the realization that you are not telling the story just to let people know about something that happened to you, but that you are setting out to offer inspiration and determination and a possible solution to other people who might be facing a similar challenge, dealing with a tragedy, or yearning to reach for a seemingly impossible goal.

The personal experience story, then, is a minidrama not unlike the longer true-life pieces, but suffused with the soul-searching that only a first-person narrator can provide. The personal essay, on the other hand, while it may use a life event as a jumping-off point, is not a drama but a "think" or opinion piece. Essays are short—three to five pages—and quite easy to write, assuming you have some talent and that you have something you are burning to say. Not much research is necessary, and the structure is largely up to you, although of course one always needs a beginning, a middle, and an end, with excellent transitions in between. Depending on your talents and state of mind, you can be humorous, angry, nostalgic, cynical, iconoclastic, outrageous, or visionary. There are many markets for essays, in magazines as well as on the Op-Ed ("opposite editorial") pages of newspapers, especially for the angry or controversial essay. *Newsweek*'s "My Turn" page is designed for this type of piece, and some monthly magazines have similar columns, such as *Gentlemen's Quarterly*'s "All about Adam," and "Reflections" in *Woman's Day*. A number of other magazines, such as *Washington Post Magazine* and *Ski*, also use personal opinion pieces, although they don't have regular columns. Check your market guides for names, addresses, and requirements.

Remember that this is one type of piece that should be sent in as a completed manuscript, both because of its brevity and the unpredictability of the genre. You could send a query letter to an editor explaining that you plan to write a sidesplittingly funny essay on do-it-yourself plumbing and carpentry disasters, but even if you started the query with a genuinely humorous lead, the editor would be hard pressed to decide whether you could keep up the wisecracking for another five pages. Similarly, you might tell an editor that you are furious about the paltry amount of government funding for the arts, but he wouldn't know whether your opinions were well founded or whether you could write persuasively. Therefore, you're better off writing the whole piece to begin with. And don't forget that here, perhaps more than with any other type of article, you should let the piece cool, and then polish it to a dazzling farethee-well before sending it in.

Incidentally, this is also a time to be prepared for rejections. Nowhere is the art of writing and the reaction of editors more subjective and less based on measurable checkpoints than with the essay. What one editor finds witty another may find offensive. Your opinion about housing for the homeless may fascinate one editor and bore another one. If you know your piece is worthy, just keep shooting it back out into the marketplace until you find an editor who agrees with you.

Essays and personal experience articles, then, are excellent vehicles for part-time writers to break into print and gain confidence; furthermore, this type of piece often remains a primary and continuing source of modest income as you add other, more lucrative forms of writing to your arsenal. A good example is how-to writing: It won't necessarily make you rich, but it can supply you with a steady flow of sales, especially in smaller markets, and give you the chance to learn about anything from food poisoning to fire prevention. Sound interesting? It is. So let's learn the how-to's of how-to writing. . . .

11

The How-To's of How-To Articles

THOUSANDS OF MAGAZINES across the country are hungry for how-to pieces that educate readers about an almost endless range of topics including gardening, home maintenance, cooking, beauty, health and fitness, fashion, automobile maintenance, carpentry, needlework and crafts, first aid, pet care and training, accident and crime prevention. Flip through the current crop of magazines on the newsstand and in the library, and you'll surely find pieces as diverse as how to arrange a funeral, what you need to know about installing locks and burglar alarm systems, how to save a choking child, the facts about buying your first home, landscaping made simple, how to pick a sweet-tempered puppy, how to cope with airline delays, and how to get the most out of your microwave. True, major magazines usually have "service" or how-to editors and writers on staff, but the vast majority of publications depend on free lancers for how-to material. What's more, editors welcome queries from beginners and part-time writers.

That's good news, but what's even better is that you don't have to be an expert on any given topic in order to write about it. In fact, lack of expertise can even be an advantage, especially if you're aiming at a general interest magazine. After all, a curious, open-minded writer who knows little about a topic will have all the same questions and problems as the uninitiated reader and, therefore, will really go after the whole story in order to come up with an excellent primer on the subject at hand.

Of course, if you *are* an expert in some field, that can be an advantage as well. You're in a position to write for the specialty markets, those that assume a certain level of basic knowledge in their readers and are thus looking for pieces that focus on a detailed aspect of the topic without going into all the basics. There are magazines for every interest and need, from *AAA World* (auto safety and driving how-to's) to *Zymurgy* (how-to's for beer lovers and homebrewers). A random sampling from the hundreds of listings in *The Writer's Handbook* includes *The American Rose Magazine* (articles on home rose gardens), *Log Home Guide* (articles on building new log homes, especially with solar or alternate heating systems), *Workbench* (how-to articles on home improvement and do-it-yourself projects), *Bassin'* (articles on how and where to bass fish), *Hot Rod* (how-to articles on auto mechanics, hot rods, track and drag racing), *New Body* (how-to's for female fitness buffs), *Moneyplan Magazine* (how-to pieces on financial planning and money management), *Alternative Energy Retailer* (for retailers of alternative energy products . . . stressing the how-to), *California Lawyer* (how-to's on improving techniques in law practice), *Christian Bookseller* (merchandising how-tos), *Flowers &* (how-to information for retail florists), *Baptist Leader* (how-to articles for lay leaders and teachers of local church education), *Instructor* (how-to articles on elementary classroom teaching), *Popular Photography* (how-to articles for amateur and professional photographers), and *Cat Fancy* (articles on cat care, health, grooming, etc.) In fact, time spent going through the pages of *The Writer's Handbook* will not only yield potential markets for your own how-to pieces, but it will also convince you that your writing *will* eventually be published. All those editors of all those magazines have lots of pages to fill, with only twenty working days a month to get any given issue published. They need you!

As always, of course, you must prepare an irresistible query letter, with evidence of your expertise or research, in order to convince these editors that they need you. Also, no matter how well versed you are in any field, whether through experience or research, your how-to pieces won't sell unless they are written in what editors call the "nuts and bolts" style—information presented with absolute clarity. This is not the place for lush and leisurely prose. Stick to the facts and instructions, which can certainly be presented in running text as in any other article, although you are best off here if you use subheads to define the sections of your outline.

How-to pieces can also have special formats, however. You can use "bullets" to set off a list of defined terms. For example, if you were doing a piece on home mortgages, you might list the following:

- **Downpayment**
A portion of the purchase price of the home, paid in a lump sum

- **Principal**
The purchase price minus the downpayment

- **Points**
Fee paid to the lender, with each point representing 1% of the principal

- **Interest**
Finance charge added to the monthly principal payment

- **Equity**
The downpayment, plus the amount of principal you have paid

You can also use numbered lists, especially for instructions that must be followed in a certain order, and you can enclose some portions of your piece in separate boxes for emphasis. Charts and graphs are other options, and of course, some how-to pieces need illustrations or photographs. You may either provide these or choose to collaborate with an artist or photographer.

The how-to field is vast, and not particularly difficult to break into. Just remember to study your target markets to see what type of service pieces they favor and to absorb the tone of their titles and leads. All in all, how-to writing can be educational and fun, a relief from the backbreaking and emotionally wearing work of some other nonfiction journalism. In the same vein, you might want to tuck in some really light and easy writing between major pieces. That's our next stop: fillers, anecdotes and other delectable, marketable morsels.

12

Filling in the Blanks

IF BREVITY IS THE SOUL OF WIT, as Shakespeare wrote, it is also the key to turning snippets of information, moments of inspiration, or humorous incidents into tidbits that will delight editors and readers alike, while keeping you penning away between major assignments. The market for fillers—hints, light verse, humorous anecdotes, quizzes and the like—is quite broad, as your market guides will reveal. Some magazines, such as *Reader's Digest*, have several departments devoted solely to these short takes (the only free-lance material *Reader's Digest* uses). Other magazines use these short items and fillers simply as a stop-gap to plug the hole when a regular story runs just short of the space allotted to it. And some publications devote one or more pages per issue to these short pieces.

In addition, some major magazines publish special sections bound into copies sent to specific regions of the country, and some have special sections for affluent subscribers, as ascertained by their zip codes. The pieces in these sections are seldom more than 750 words long, and are often as short as 100 or 200 words; yet the spectrum of what is published is as varied as what goes into the regular pages, if not more so.

Beyond this, virtually all magazines use some type of filler material. A quick look at *The Writer's Handbook* reveals that fillers are being sought by the editors of a host of publications, including *The American Newspaper Carrier, Army Magazine, Bird Watcher's Digest, Cashflow, Down East, Expecting, Golf Digest, Modern Maturity, Northwest Living, Volkswagen's World*, and on and on and on! Also, study magazines in the library and on the newsstands to uncover countless markets for your anecdotes, verse, puzzles, and hints. Usually, magazines don't acknowledge or return fillers, so after about 90 days, you can assume you're free to submit your work elsewhere. It's a good idea to keep a flow chart if you're going to be doing a lot of filler writing.

The techniques for producing short pieces are the same as those for researching and writing longer stories, except that you must learn to present your information in a concentrated form. Let me help you by telling you what I have learned about writing several specialized types of miniature masterpieces, which, not surprisingly, are harder to create than they seem to be:

• Helpful hints

Club soda will take the stains out of your kitchen counter and your clothes . . . Putting damp cotton garments into a self-seal plastic bag and freezing before ironing makes wrinkles disappear easily . . . . Squirting naughty cats with a child's water pistol will teach them to stop clawing furniture or using the foyer as a litter box. These are but a few of the pieces of information I've learned over the years as a filler writer and editor. But I've also learned that hint writing, like most any other kind, must be both lively and accurate. Suppose you wanted to explain how to use worn-out toothbrushes as household cleaning tools. You could be dry and uninspired and simply say:

> Put cleanser on worn-out toothbrushes to scrub tile, dishwasher buttons, and faucets.

No one will pay you even $25 for that bloodless bit of prose. But what about this?

> Give an aging toothbrush a new career! Those past-their-prime bristles work perfectly on such hard-to-reach places as the greenish grout between bathtub tiles, the secret scum collections behind appliance buttons and the rusty rings around kitchen and bathroom faucets. Just moisten the brush, dab on a little cleanser and scrub away. Voilà! The grime is gone, and you didn't spend a penny on special tools.

On the other hand, you don't want to sacrifice clarity for cuteness when your tip deals with something as serious as investing money or saving someone's life. For example, if you were writing about sunstroke, you'd do best to be absolutely straightforward:

> Sunstroke is serious, especially in young children. Symptoms include flushed, dry skin, absence of sweating, and high temperature. First, get the victim in out of the sun and call for medical help, then lower body temperature by placing the victim in a tub of cool water and sponging briskly, or by wrapping the victim in cold, wet sheets. Do not give stimulants.

● **Humorous anecdotes**

Funny little pieces taken from real-life incidents—the sort of stories you might see in *Reader's Digest*'s "Life in These United States"—are found in many other magazines, as well: *Alcoholism & Addiction Magazine* has a "Coffee Break Page" for anecdotes; *Catholic Digest* has "In Our Parish"; *South Florida* Magazine has "Undercurrents"; and *Road King* has a "Trucker's Life" section. And many, many magazines without special anecdote sections scatter anecdotes throughout their pages. Again, study the markets. But remember, what sends one editor into paroxysms of laughter may leave another editor cold. Even so, there are certain guidelines that can help you figure out what is most likely to make the average editor chuckle—and send you a check.

First of all, an incident in which the joke is on someone innocent or helpless—a child, a sweet little old lady, a handicapped person—is probably not going to get you anywhere. I used to edit

LHJ's "Out of the Mouths of Babes" section, which is supposed to be rib-tickling ripostes uttered by little kids, and I was constantly amazed at how many would-be contributors, usually parents and grandparents, thought it was cute to mislead and misinform children, and then to laugh at the youngsters' confusion. For some reason, these were most frequently about sexuality and religion. Countless people, I have learned, will tell a two-year-old that swallowing an apple seed will cause a tree to grow in his stomach, and then find it hilarious when the child asks what kind of seed Mommy swallowed to make the baby grow in her tummy. Many other people will explain to a three-year-old that God looks down on her from a window in heaven, and then laugh when the child, underfoot during spring cleaning, asks whether God has Windex in heaven. I'm not saying that's not funny. I'm laughing about it right now and you probably are, too. The point is that most editors refuse to publish cruel anecdotes that make fun of people's inadequacies or disabilities or try to make readers laugh at someone else's expense. They also reject humor that is tasteless, lewd, or pokes fun at any ethnic group.

What *is* funny to most magazine editors, then? You're best off looking for incidents in which the humor stems from a very young child's own delightful misinterpretation of the world, or from an older child's or an adult's intentional parry of wit. Coincidence can also be funny—the unexpected, the element of surprise that hits the funnybone. But whatever humorous situation you choose to write about, use all the care you would in crafting a major story. Here, as anywhere, you need structure with transitions, and because the writing is so tight, every word must get you where you're going—to the punch line, of course. If writing humorous anecdotes sounds like something you'd like to try, spend some time in the library reading a lot of them, and photocopy your favorites to use as models back home.

● **Light verse**

This is simply humor that rhymes, and what makes the verse funny is that it deals with painfully prevalent human foibles and mishaps, showing the reader that he is not alone, and letting him have a gentle little laugh at himself. Good topics might be best-laid plans gone awry, finally organizing one's desk and then not being able to find anything, diet failure, coping with toddlers indoors on a rainy day, household appliances that refuse to work when one needs them most, getting lost trying to follow someone's directions, cleaning up the kitchen after Dad and the kids have cooked breakfast on Mother's Day, saving coupons and forgetting to redeem them, finding Easter grass behind the couch when you're vacuuming up the needles from the Christmas tree (or the other way around), and breaking New Year's resolutions.

Once you've settled on a topic, you need to know how to write a sprightly little verse that scans *perfectly,* in the relentless rhythm characteristic of this form (and incidentally, of greeting cards, as well). Believe me, as the former editor of *LHJ*'s "Last Laughs" column, I can tell you that there is a genuine need for writers who can turn out these funny verses. In fact, there was such a dearth of them in the slush mail that I often wrote them myself under the pen name of Corrine Clements. Here's a trio of my contributions, to get you thinking:

ANIMAL ANTICS
Raccoons in the garbage pail
Sparrows in the eaves
Squirrels in the attic—
Those are *my* pet peeves.

THE NEW ROMANCE
He did the dishes and put them away.
He got the kids all to sleep. (Hurray!)
He didn't bring bonbons or flowers or wine—
But this man is *my* kind of St. Valentine!

LIGHTS, CAMERA, ACTION
How charming are the little ones
Upon this Christmas morn!
How gracious, too, the grownups
As bows and wraps are torn!
Is it the season's spirit
That accounts for such good cheer?
No. It's Dad recording live on tape
What's going on this year.

In addition to the short takes I've just discussed, there are also jokes, humor lists modeled after the "Murphy's Law" concept, quizzes, puzzles, horoscopes, Q. and A. pieces, and inspirational or religious verse. Fortified with what I've told you thus far about filler writing in general, and humor in particular, you can simply find examples of whichever of these you'd like to write and learn from the models.

That about wraps it up, as far the techniques and types of nonfiction go. But there's one more crucial skill you need to know if you're not only going to break into the article-writing business, but *stay* there: how to work well with magazine editors. That's the last lesson I have for you. Don't skip it. Take heed, and learn it well.

≋ 13

Working with Magazine Editors

Remember that wonderful editor at *Today's Parents* magazine who gave you the "go-head on spec" for your piece on helping children cope with the loss of loved ones? Let's say that you wrote back, agreeing to do the piece within six weeks. Then you did your research and interviews, wrote your article, let it cool for a while and did some self-editing. You made sure—

- all facts were accurate.
- all experts were properly identified.
- all medical, legal and other "expert" terms were clearly defined.
- complete information was included throughout—ages, names, motivation for actions, anything that an editor or reader might wonder about if it were omitted.
- your transitions were smooth.
- you had varied your sentence structure.
- key words had not been repeated too often, and if they had, you got out your thesaurus, and substituted synonyms.

You also—

- proofread meticulously, then corrected typographical errors, grammar, and spelling mistakes.
- made a clean print-out with a fresh ribbon in your printer (or retyped the piece, whichever).

Triumphantly, you popped the manuscript—plus a courteous, brief cover letter, a bibliography, and a list of sources for fact checking—into a large envelope and sent the article off to meet its fate.

Now what? Any number of scenarios could evolve at this point, but one thing is certain. Your work is not over yet, as we shall see. At a major national magazine, it could be that the editor has been hoping to use your piece for a particular issue, and so he eagerly rips open the envelope when it arrives, reads the story on the spot, and is thrilled with the professional job you've done. He passes the manuscript on to the editor-in-chief with a glowing note that finishes with, "I'd buy right away." The editor-in-chief drops everything, devours your story, and routes it right back with a note saying, "Yes, buy immediately and run in next issue." (Monthly magazines have a "lead time" of three months, meaning that the piece submitted and accepted in May can run in August at the earliest.) The editor will then either write or phone you. If he does the latter, let's hope that he reaches you directly or that you have a functioning telephone answering machine. There is nothing more annoying to a busy major magazine editor than futile attempts to get in touch with writers. Even if all he wants at this point is to congratulate you and ask you for your Social Security number, he'd like to be able to leave word and know that you'll get back to him as soon as possible, which is what the cordial message on your answering machine ought to convey.

But at the average or smaller publications and even at major magazines, the pleasant picture I've just painted, in which the editor wants to buy and run your piece immediately, is not the usual one. Maybe the editor-in-chief doesn't need your piece for the next issue, and he puts off reading it for days or even weeks while he handles more pressing matters. Also, whenever he gets around to reading your story, he may find problems with your structure or your choice of lead and want revisions. He may feel you've used too little dialogue or he may have read something in the paper about new research which he feels you ought to include. Depending on the extent of the changes and additions required, you will be asked to do minor revisions and make changes, or to do a heavy rewrite. Just be glad your piece wasn't rejected altogether, and vow to do whatever you can to help the editor make the article a winner. Remember, you and the editor are in this together, and both of you want exactly the same thing: an excellent finished article.

Now you've made your changes or done your rewrite and at long last, the piece has been ac-

cepted. At this point, the article might simply be
filed in the magazine's inventory for use in a future issue, especially if the topic is what editors
call an "evergreen," one that will stay fresh or
need only minimal updating. Or the piece may be
scheduled for a certain issue and then get
"bumped," either because the size of the issue was
changed on account of last-minute additions or
reductions in advertising pages, or because the
editors needed space for a more timely article, or
simply because the editor-in-chief had a change of
mind (whether capricious or judicious) about the
mix of articles in that issue. Should any of these
events take place, do not whine to your editor.
Editors work as a team, and while your editor
may sympathize with your eagerness to see your
name in print, he alone does not have the final say
as to when that day will come.

Eventually, though, your story will be scheduled. In the largest magazines, either the articles
editor or another person (variously called a text
editor or a line editor) will work on your manuscript from then on. At smaller magazines, the
line-editing is done along with copy-editing by the
same person you've been working with all along.
In either case, the editor will fine-tune the piece
and may call you now and then with questions.
Again, be quick about getting any information the
editor needs, whether it's one more crucial quote
from a case history person or a better definition of
a disease. I'm not saying there is no room for

discussion here. You can politely and intelligently talk about points with your line editor. But try to give the editors what they want if the requests are at all reasonable—and they probably are.

After the piece has been line-edited and approved, it will go into production. By now, the art department will have created a layout. Your line editor may have to change the title to fit the design, and he may be writing a blurb or two (those one- or two-sentence flags in large type that catch the readers' attention), maybe some "pull quotes" (excerpts from your piece, repeated in large type—also called "bump up quotes"), plus subheads, picture captions, and a blurb for the table of contents. In most (if not all) cases, you will not be consulted at all about these items.

In the case of the major magazines, you will usually receive an edited version of your article for approval. You will need to read it immediately and phone or write in any changes. At this point (again, only on the larger national magazines), you may also hear from the fact-checker if he is having trouble reaching one of your experts or understanding a reference.

Then the day of the "close" will arrive. Because of space limitations, your line editor may have to cut or add lines, especially if there are "widows" (an incomplete line at the top of a new page or column). There is usually no time to consult the author at this stage, since the adjusted piece is by then pasted onto "boards" or "mechanicals" as camera-ready copy and is ready to be sent to the printer. However, no *major* changes will be made without contacting the author.

Well, you did it. You broke into article writing. In a few weeks or months, you'll get your advance sample copies of the issue to prove it. When you do, you'll surely flip the magazine open to the table of contents, and savor the sight of your by-line. Then you'll turn to your piece, and experience the thrill of reading your own words from the printed page. It doesn't matter whether you broke into a major national magazine or a smaller, specialized publication. What does matter is that you really are a published writer.

Best of all, you know that your success was not a fluke. You've begun to learn the art and craft of nonfiction writing, and you've behaved in a responsible and businesslike manner. There will be both rejections and acceptances in your future, of course. But you sold once, and you can do it again—and again, and again. Congratulations, and welcome aboard!